Poetry
By Me And
My Family

About
Art, Science, Love & Life

Ronald J. Yadusky, BS, MD, FACS

authorHOUSE®

AuthorHouse™
1663 Liberty Drive
Bloomington, IN 47403
www.authorhouse.com
Phone: 1-800-839-8640

Published by AuthorHouse 2/29/2012

ISBN: 978-1-4685-5715-2 (e)
ISBN: 978-1-4685-5716-9 (hc)
ISBN: 978-1-4685-5717-6 (sc)

Library of Congress Control Number: 2012903701

This book is printed on acid-free paper.

Because of the dynamic nature of the Internet, any web addresses or links contained in this book may have changed since publication and may no longer be valid. The views expressed in this work are solely those of the author and do not necessarily reflect the views of the publisher, and the publisher hereby disclaims any responsibility for them.

Dedication

I dedicate this book to God, and to my dear wife, Margaret, who is a cherished gift of God to me. I love her dearly and always will, and similarly I love my five children, living and dead: Mary, Joseph, William, John and Ann; and their families, as well as mine and Margaret's.

Acknowledgements

Isaac Newton (English physicist, Astronomer, 1643-1727) said that the reason we see so far is because we stand on the shoulders of giants. I thank all the giants on whose shoulders I stand—namely: my wife Margaret, family, teachers, preachers, authors, mentors, and examples that have guided me to this point.

Many thanks and heartfelt gratitude to my proofreaders for their caring interest and help with this work: Mary Galligan, Claire Galligan, Craig and Ann Barta, Christina Barta, Jessica Barta, Jonathan Barta, Joe and Laura Yadusky, Sally Yadusky, Megan Yadusky, Sarah Yadusky, Jacob Yadusky, William (Will) Yadusky, Kaye Yadusky, William and Katie Yadusky, Aleksandra Yadusky, Catherine Staton, Donald and Joan Yadusky, Katie Gold, Kit and Stephanie Cessna, Rachel Cessna, Hunter Cessna, Dan and Julianne Brunson, Anna Katherine Brunson, Peter Yadusky, Scott Yadusky, John Patani, Charles Frederick IV (Chip) and Kim Colvin, Charles Frederick V (Charlie) Colvin, Andrew John Colvin, Grace Margaret Colvin, Sherri and Sabrina Dodd Tumicelli, Nikolas Devon Dodd, Mikhael Gavin Dodd, Catrina Van Diest, Mary (Pete) Troy, Brenda and Joel Clayton, Barnwell Ray and Emma Stone (Rocky) Beard, Cindy and George Patrick, Fay Crouch, Rita Brunson, Marcelo and Nina Alvarez, Gia Alvarez, Jane Black, Paul Bartley, Tom and Grace Hughes.

Special thanks and gratitude, also, to my pastor of St. Mary Magdalene Church, **Reverend Father Donald Staib**, who thought that this collection of poems surely took a good bit of effort and creativity. It made him reflect that the words of poetry are somewhat different from the way of communication by words, gestures and facial expressions. Sometimes we speak hastily or use an unfortunate word or expression, and wish we could take it back. But words get out there and stay like the air in our environment. Poetic words are carefully thought out and compared with other words. And they are sometimes changed and improved, because we want those words to express a deeper thought, and a more accurate portrayal of our feelings, love, sorrow, disappointment and admiration. Older folks may remember lyrics of the 1986 song, "Words" (songwriters Barry Gibb, Robin Gibb, Maurice Ernest Gibb) of the Bee Gees: "It's only words, and words are all I have, to take your heart away."

Special thanks and gratitude, also, to artist **Kit Cessna** for pencil drawings throughout this book that exemplify his artistic talent. He retired from the U.S. Army in 1994. While on active duty, he served with C-Squadron Delta, 1st Special Forces Group, and the 2nd Ranger Battalion.

Kit held a reserve commission with the Baton Rouge Police Department primarily serving on the Special Response team. In 2000, he was shot in the line of duty during a hostage barricade. For this operation and other services provided to the department, he was named Police Officer of the Year for 2000.

Later, commissioned as a reserve deputy for the East Baton Rouge Parish Sheriff's Office, Kit was part of the SWAT response into New Orleans in the aftermath of Hurricane Katrina.

Currently he is an instructor for the U.S. Department of State Anti-Terrorism Assistance Program, the Southern Anti-Terrorist Regional Training Academy, and Louisiana State University Weapons of Mass Destruction Program.

Kit is the author of two books: "All Enemies Foreign and Domestic" and "Equal or Greater Force." And he has contributed two essay articles that make up half of chapter 6 in the expanded edition of the second edition of the book "Warriors," in which top warriors in the country were invited to contribute by the editor Loren W. Christensen.

Omaha Beach, Day 2
All were called to give some, some were called to give all.
(Art by artist Kit Cessna 2011)

Note

Let me explain the letters after my name:

B.S. for graduating from Villanova University with a Bachelor of Science degree in pre-med.

M.D. for graduating from Jefferson Medical University.

F.A.C.S. for going through a surgical residency program and becoming a Fellow of the American College of Surgeons.

My internship was one year at Fitzgerald Mercy Hospital in Darby, Pennsylvania.

My residency program was four years of General Surgery at Lankenau Hospital in Overbrook, Pennsylvania and two years of Thoracic and Cardiovascular Surgery at the Berthold S. Pollak Hospital of Chest Diseases in Jersey City, New Jersey, followed by a year of Cardiovascular Surgery Research Fellowship.

I'm Board Certified in both General Surgery and Thoracic and Cardiovascular Surgery.

Contents

v   Dedication
vii   Acknowledgements
xi   Note
xxi   Images
xxiii Introduction

Art

2   Self-Portrait
       Poets Have That Same Right Too

3   A Story Needs Balance
       A Happy Ending

4   Choice
       Your Choice

5   There's More I Need
       Poets Take Heed

6   Be Poet Enough
       Correct Your View

9   Do My Words Rhyme?
       Free Verse Needn't Rhyme

10   A Third Way
       Combined Completeness

12   Synthesis
       Duality To Trinity

14   Duality Has Two Sides
       Feel The Pendulum's Pull

16   See And Say
       The Urge To Be Heard

18   Haunted By Restlessness
Catching God's Spark

20   Truth
There's Lots Of It

21   God Is An Artist
Understanding Suffering

22   The Nutcracker
Christmas Ballet

24   Ride The Flow
A Lot Of Rhyme To Take

25   It
Making Use Of It

26   That
Not This, But That

27   Plots
Not A Submarine

28   That Comes Before It
That's Not It

30   The potential of language
Truth, Justice and Change

32   Big Words
Pretentious

34   Poetical Without Rhyme
Free Verse

36   The Sky At Night
Variegated Fascination

38   Alliteration
Getting Out "D" Word

Science

44   Diamonds
         What's Better

46   Fool's Gold
         Gold Fever

48   Anatomy
         A Privilege

50   Neutrinos
         Ghost Particles

52   Mathematics
         Many Branches

54   Minimally Invasive Surgery
         VATS

56   Sand
         Arenology

58   Reboot For Mood Upgrade
         Technology

60   Stem Cells
         Help May Cause Harm

61   Three Things Can Relate
         Physics Theory

64   Quantum Dimensions
         Trying To Keep Count

66   Tin, Gin & Uranium
         Oh Brother!

67   Computer Language
         Old Words Have New Meanings

68   Unintended Consequence
Collateral Damage

70   Nothing
Zero

72   Pi
A Constant

74   Quadrivium
Ancient Curriculum

75   Jewel thieves
Real Treasure

Love

80   Surgeons Display A Love That's Deep
Little Things Distract From Big

82   Secret Agent
One Unburnt Bridge

83   Your Favorite
Ice Cream

84   More Than Defenses
Love Is The Goal

86   Trouble in the Home
Who's To Blame?

87   Surrounded by Love
Awareness

90   Graduation
My Final One Is Near

92   Christmas Is A Birthday (1)
Christ is in Christmas (1)

94   Christmas Is A Birthday (2)
       Christ Is In Christmas (2)

96   Free Verse
       Love Rhymes

98   Love Draws
       So Find It

100   A Ring
       You Are Beloved

102   Leading Like New Stars
       Love Needs An Other

104   Adventure Or Romance
       Live To Love

106   Can We Just Talk A While?
       I Hear You're Seeking Me

108   There's A Way To Know
       All This Is Proof

110   Shoved By A Kiss
       Sexual Desire Fire

Life

113   People Poke And Pratfall
       Laughter

114   Pushing The Envelope
       But It's Stationery

115   Experience
       Beauty Is Not Known By Proxy

116   It's Been Said
       Memorable

118   Surviving Inflation
The Rich Man Turned Away

120   Retirement Or Re-tirement
Rest Or Re-creation

121   Haunted House In The Woods
A Campfire Tale

124   Two Categories
Being Labeled

126   Picture A Time
A Missing Link

127   On The Brink
What I Think

128   Resolve To Revolve
Feel The Wheel

130   Three Watches
It's All Downhill

131   School Supplies
Home With A Fever

132   Oil, Dollars, and Real Value
Stagflation

134   A Good Guy's Hat
Good Example To See

135   Beautiful Human Flowers
All They Can Be

136   We All Need Mercy
Wrath's Not A Path

138   Eat Right Or You'll Be Left
Passing On

139   Humor
          Joie de Vivre

140   Rock
          Where To Build

142   A Sinner
          Trying to Bless

144   The Story Of A Well
          A Close Encounter

145   Greed
          Being Blunt

Poems By My Family

148   Carnival Lights   Claire Holahan
          Daydreams

149   Dream   Rachel Cessna

150   How Can I Describe   Rachel Cessna

152   Spring Sing   Rachel Cessna

153   Pond Haiku   Rachel Cessna

154   Snowflakes   Christina Barta

155   Winter's Confetti   Christina Barta

156   Snow Day   Jessica Barta

157   My Poem   Jonathan Barta

158   Bon Voyage   Joseph Yadusky
          Your Ship Has Come In

159   Some Days   Sarah Yadusky

160   Remember   Sarah Yadusky

161	Beautiful Water	Sarah Yadusky
162	Friends Make The World Go Round	Sarah Yadusky
163	Franklin Haiku	William Yadusky Sr.
164	Poster Child	William Yadusky Jr.
166	Visage	William Yadusky Jr.
168	Haiku	Mary Galligan
169	Undertaking	Kaye Yadusky
170	The Ash Tree	Kaye Yadusky
172	Interview	Aleksandra Yadusky
173	Untitled-1	Alexandra Yadusky
174	Untitled-2	Aleksandra Yadusky
175	Sweet Dreams	Megan Yadusky
176	Baby Birds	Megan Yadusky
177	Moon Tales	Scott Yadusky
178	Recipe for a Peaceful Moment	Ann Barta
180	For My Teachers Who Are So Amazing!	Stephanie Cessna
181	Baseball	Jacob Yadusky

Images

ix   Omaha Beach, Day 2
          (Art by artist Kit Cessna 2011)

xxii   Family Photo

xxviii   Taking a break
          (Art by artist Kit Cessna 2011)

8   Captain Robert E. Lee
          Mexican War 1836
          (Art by artist Kit Cessna 2011)

40   Family gathering at my 80th Birthday Party

11   Grandchildren Outside The Museum

76   The Gray Wolf
          (Art by artist Kit Cessna 2012)

77   Family Gathered At A North Carolina Museum

112   Beloved

146   30,000 Feet Over Germany
          20 minutes to target
          (Art by artist Kit Cessna 2010)

Family Photo

Introduction

I believe that the purpose of all poetry is to make the world better. And I believe that after you read this book of poems, you too will be better for it.

Creativity is very personal. Some ideas for poems came to me when I was half-way between asleep and awake. Such as the poems: "Self-Portrait," "Choice" and "There's More I Need." Other poems came to me from hearing a single short catch phrase like a single short idea. Such as the poems: "Be Poet Enough" and "School Supplies." Some poems came after reading a book about the subject. Such as the poems: "Mathematics," "Nothing (Zero)" and "Pi." Other poems came from my background as a surgeon or my hobby as a rock hound. Such as the poems: "Surgeons Display A Love That's Deep," "Anatomy," "Diamonds" and "Jewel Thieves." Other poems came simply from the inspiration to write them at the time or from my spirituality. But the majority of the poems came subtly from my memoir, and directly out of my life and my love for my wife, children and family.

After publishing my memoir as a book entitled, "The Truth Collector, " in 2009 through Authorhouse Publishers in honor of my beloved wife, Margaret, who died in 2008 from cancer, I continued to be very prolific and creatively driven until I composed 67 poems that were published in 2010 in a book entitled "Poems About Art, Science, Love & Life" by Authorhouse Publishers. Now, in 2012, this present book entitled, "Poetry by Me and My Family," published by Authorhouse Publishers, represents a continuation of my poetic burst of creativity. What makes this third book different from my second is the addition of some wonderfully creative poems written by some of my family that are included.

Poetry runs in my family. The will to create and the will to love are one. Art makes love visible, and by doing so it uplifts and heals, because in the presence of love everything is healed. Creative artists just need to express freely what they see through their loving inner eyes without keeping anything hidden or suppressed. Our inner eyes can see invisible things, such as, truth, love and goodness.

Like all human beings, poets have three outstanding qualities that we call intellectual, emotional and spiritual. We find the world to be full of thinking minds, feeling emotions, and reverent spirits. The mind seeks truth, the heart seeks love, and the spirit seeks goodness and God. Beauty is found in that truth, love and goodness.

Poets by using language paint word pictures of that inner vision that, in addition to being musically and lyrically phrased, gives finite form to the infinite. Poets say tangibly what they feel intangibly. They depict in words what they see by their inner eyes, so their word pictures can be viewed by someone else's inner eyes. Poets do with words what artists do with paint, namely, create pictures for themselves and others to see. All poems influence in some way by bringing something to life.

Poets transmit the state of their being into their art. Their state of consciousness, emotions, and spirituality all get embedded into each of their works, because all art is autobiographical. Poems, also, represent something of the times in which the artist lives, and what is in those times that is psychological, political, spiritual, philosophical, social, technical, and economic. All of this gets subtly reflected in the poet's work. This is true for painting as well as for poetry.

Poets see traces of power and spirit in reality. That, plus the power of spirit found within the real poet, gives reality to the power of spirit found in their work. Art is more ideals than ideas.

Poets see not only what is visible by their physical eyes, but also, what is invisible or spiritual by what they see through their inner eyes, which we call, "eyes of their hearts." In other words, poets are always keenly aware of the difference between secular and sacred. Some prefer to call it perceptive knowledge of both the profane and the divine.

We consider poetry beautiful, because it contains truth, love and goodness, which are found in mind, heart and spirit. Also, poetry has within it a symmetry, harmony, rhythm, proportion, and perspective, which we call beautiful, and which adds to that beauty, and to the beauty that's found in the eye of the beholder.

We know art when we see it; we know truth when we hear it; we know love when we experience it; we know goodness when we find it, and we know beauty when we're confronted by it.

Godfrey Harold Hardy (British mathematician, 1877-1947) said: "The mathematician's patterns, like the painter's or the poet's must be beautiful; the ideas, like the colors or the words, must fit together in a harmonious way. Beauty is the first test: there is no permanent place in this world for ugly mathematics." Also, there is no permanent place in this world for ugly poetry. If poetry does not make us better or the world better, then, for what is it?

Beauty is important for scientists, as well as for artists, poets and mathematicians. Henri Poincare (French mathematician, theoretical physicist and philosopher of science, 1854-1912) wrote: "The scientist does not study nature because it is useful; he studies it because he delights in it, and he delights in knowing. And if nature were not worth knowing, life would not be worth living." Albert Einstein (German theoretical physicist 1879-1955) felt that a theory didn't have to be correct, as long as it was beautiful in its simplicity, because later, that theory is likely to be found true.

If you equate beauty with the visible physical body, or with the invisible feeling of knowing beauty when you see it, because you just feel it as known, then to feel beauty is to know the truth, and to know the truth is to be in love. Pope John Paul II (1920-2005) said, "Love increases by means of truth, and love draws near by means of truth."

Daily life is a paradox between knowing that you can't love what you don't know, and knowing that you only truly know that which you have fallen in love with.

Little by little, love's presence helps the artist find essence, and then the artist's poem, or art, has something to say. It tells of the artist, and if they pray. We all are artists with no paint, because each action of our lives is symbolically like the slash of a brush, or the stroke of a pen, whereby we want to show a Saint.

Since God is love, then all art, including poetry, which causes us to feel love, is really showing us the face of God. Poetry at its highest really proves the existence of God. Art that does not cause us to feel love, or to see God, misses the true full potential of art

Poems invite, inform and inspire. They invite, because, like beauty, they are attractive. They inform, because they have something to say. And they inspire, because we are touched and moved by them. We slow down in reading poems, because poetic words give us something worth savoring in terms of truth, love, goodness, beauty, poignancy, etc. We are taken in and held by the poem's momentum and focus. Some would argue that punctuation is not needed in poetry, but when properly used, punctuation is like adding pepper or salt to food. In that sense, it tends to complete it.

Poets are aware that what's been going on in the universe for billions of years is a cosmic and biologic diversity with evolution. Nothing is accidental, because there's a continual perfect balance of evolving forces and tensions. Artists align themselves with this unfolding design of universal creativity, cosmic scale, infinite diversity and divine intelligence. Human consciousness is a complex part of this. Language is used as a tool by the mind to make our intelligence reasonable. Spiritual practice is also a tool. And we use that tool to gain access to the transrational state or supernatural, which is very personal, and is depicted in personal poems.

Poems bring us into personal contact with that creative spirit, which is divinely beautiful, noble, honorable and true. Such contact gives us a chance, not only, for self discovery, but for collective change as well. When the poets express themselves, their poems mirror our world, or tell us of new worlds. Their poems show to us our spiritual potential, our ability to be transformed, and the sacredness present in life. If we cannot envision a better world, we cannot create one. You will find yourself torn between wanting to save the world and wanting to savor it. If the spiritual is not known to an artist, then what that artist shows in their art is a representation of what is either unknown or what is a lie.

There is no higher goal for art than to heal, bless, bring to life, catalyze the world's spiritual evolution, and honor the values that make life worth living. When love reaches a critical mass, the world will experience a radical shift. Poets put into poems their own will, plus the divine will. If they don't, they lose meaning and the art of seeing. Failing to include both means a poet's words will produce works without meaning, and show a world that is meaningless, even though some meaning of a piece of art is found in those who look upon the work. Ultimate meaning points to God, the source of unique beauty, truth, and goodness. St. Augustine (Bishop, Doctor of the Church, 354-430) said, "Our whole business in this life is to restore to health the eye of the heart whereby God may be seen." Oscar Wilde (Irish writer and poet, 1854-1900) said: "One does not see anything until one sees its beauty." Poems show outer beauty and inner radiance. Poems show the external and the internal essence and spirit. Creation is defined in the same way that we define art, namely, spirit expressed into matter. Poetry at its essence depicts a spiritual world.

Poets have keen vision and sensitive feeling for all of ordinary life. Poets can hear the grass grow and the squirrel's heartbeat, and they die from that roar, (that loud sound), on the other side of silence. Love is the loudest sound on the other side of silence.

Thank you for your interest. God bless you. Please enjoy these poems. Ron

Taking a break
(Art by artist Kit Cessna 2011)

Art

Self-Portrait
Poets Have That Same Right Too

(Written in a meter of .-.-.-.-.-)
Iambic Pentameter
10 syllables in 20 rhyming lines

My name is Doctor Ronald Yadusky,
And I'm a poet who writes poetry.
Self-portraits are what painters get to do.
I think all poets have that same right too.
 My memoir has been published in a book.
 It's there for you, and you can take a look.
 The book's entitled "The Truth Collector,"
 Available from any good book store.
My book will show you that I'm so much more.
A life as surgeon is there at my core.
I'm also brother, husband, and I'm dad,
Uncle, grandpa, and widower who's sad.
 Perhaps these facts do not mean much to you,
 But I have saved some lives a time or two.
 I'm now retired, but keeping you in view.
 You'll find my writings can move & change you.
What's moving is not when some actors cry,
But when the audience cries itself dry.
And poet's words don't move when being said,
They move when heard and understood, instead.

A Story Needs Balance
A Happy Ending

(Written in a meter of .-.-.-.-)
Iambic Tetrameter
8 syllables in 20 rhyming lines

A story must have unity,
Although divided into three:
beginning, middle and an end.
Its conflict-cycles rise in trend.
 The cycles, and their trend, need this,
 A balance, or they'll be remiss,
 For both exist and want more say.
 Both balanced is the best third way.
A pendulum in cycles swings,
Returning to important things.
But trends they have trajectory.
They can move indefinitely.
 There is a trend called, "certain trend."
 It makes a stop and has an end.
 But sex trend, even at its peak,
 Resists a stop with more to seek
A happy ending it needs this,
The balance of a boy and miss.
Because of love they'll both submit
To care forever and commit.

Choice
Your Choice

(Written in a meter of .-.-.-.-.-)
Iambic Pentameter
10 syllables in 16 rhyming lines

All words you hear are either false or true.
To sort it out is something you must do.
For truth must always be for you the Boss,
'Cause what is false will always lead to loss.
    But what is real can never be unreal.
    Distinction here is really a big deal,
    Because unreal may sometimes feel like real.
    Each day brings choices, even for each meal.
A choice means that from two you must choose one.
Some choices will seem easy and be fun,
But other times you won't know what to say.
In times like that you just will have to pray.
    Thank God you've chosen now to read my book,
    To open it to give yourself a look.
    I pray that as you read you'll sense God's voice
    To urge you to keep reading this, your choice.

There's More I Need
Poets Take Heed

Written in a meter of .-.-.-.-)
Iambic Tetrameter
8 syllables in 16 rhyming lines

Don't talk of garden's sweet flowers,
Or weather that may bring showers.
I want to know about my life,
And why I have to have such strife.
    Some metaphors are very nice,
    But daily I must pay the price
    For being immature and dumb.
    My own mistakes keep me quite numb.
So, poets, if you care, take heed.
Put in your poems what I need.
Enlighten, lift and instruct me.
I sense there's more that I should see.
    I fear, if you'll give what I ask,
    I may not be up to the task
    To change into what I should be,
    Despite the help that you'll give me.

Be Poet Enough
Correct Your View

(Written in a meter of .-.-.-.-.-)
Iambic Pentameter
10 syllables in 32 alternately rhyming lines

Be poet enough to correct your view.
Just really look to see things as they are:
Life growing up and flourishing anew,
While truth and love and goodness are not far.
    Some only see reeds shaken by the wind,
    Without a purpose or a goal, or zeal.
    Such folks have a lot they'd like to rescind,
    But there's much more to think and see and feel.
So, if you truly can begin to see,
You'll see how life is blind without a rhyme.
And how there is much more for us to be,
For poets see beyond both space and time.
    Be poet enough to correct your life.
    Try hard to understand another one,
    And bring some riches out despite the strife.
    Look into your own heart to get that done.
And love can strike you from out of the blue,
For it is something that's beyond control.
True love puts romance into helpless you,
Because to fall in love it makes you whole.
    And when you fall in love, you will learn more
    Than what you ever thought you knew before.
    Because, when someone you love and adore
    Returns that love, it will affect your core.
And life will come together in your view.
You'll feel that what you knew will all be new.
Be poet enough to see that is true,
And start correcting what you need to do.

A single flower is a mystery,
That's how things are intended just to be.
You can proceed when you don't have a clue,
When love tells you exactly what to do.

Captain Robert E. Lee
Mexican War 1836
(Art by artist Kit Cessna 2011)

Do My Words Rhyme?
Free Verse Needn't Rhyme

(Written in a meter of .-.-.-.-)
Iambic Tetrameter
8 syllables in 20 rhyming lines

The words I say they may not rhyme,
'Cause I can never find the time
To think about such things, you know.
But otherwise my words can flow.
    So why do you call me "poet"?
    I need to know the "why" of it .
    Please listen to just how I talk,
    And then perhaps you'll start to balk.
For I can't see that words from me
Are spoken poetically.
The only thing that I do know
Is free verse needn't rhyme; that's so.
    And poems, also, are like ash
    From burning lives that have panache.
    Do you think I've some dash and verve?
    To write in rhyme seems to take nerve.
I could be wrong, 'cause that's my thing.
Poems are worth remembering.
So I'll use verse to say much more
Than my prose words have said before.

A Third Way
Combined Completeness

(Written in a meter of .-.-.-.-.-)
Iambic Pentameter
10 syllables in 40 rhyming lines

I do believe the Pharaohs all had meant
To be united in one government.
The purpose and the goal of that intent
Was for a kind of "Promised Land" event,
    Which then would stand as a great metaphor,
    Uniting what was separate before.
    The Nile Valley had Upper and Lower
    Divided kingdoms of "two lands" power.
To integrate the two would make "third land."
A chance for betterment seemed close at hand.
The symbol "three" showed a more perfect way.
Uniting still prevails for us today.
    In marriage male and female are "third way."
    "Uniting *yin* and *yang*," the Chinese say,
    Which is a unity that does express
    Completeness, wholeness and a new oneness.
Let's synthesize what is diversity
To form a "child" that's born with certainty.
I think that's what all artists want and wish.
Uniting contrasts isn't outlandish.
    We all want to: unite both life and death;
    Give old and new philosophy new breath:
    Find balance and new paths for us to see,
    And reconcile combined duality.
For wholes are greater than sums of each part.
Beyond all knowledge wisdom does impart.
I know that's what you want, and how you've felt.
You want united merging to get melt.

Put sodium in water it explodes.
The element called chlorine it erodes.
Combine these both together and you'll get
The nourishing salt of earth, don't forget.
And everything in moderation's right.
In paradox a third way's kept in sight.
And "Virtue's in the middle," that's expressed.
Out of the good and better comes the best.

Synthesis
Duality To Trinity

(Written in a meter of .-.-.-)
Iambic Tetrameter
8 syllables in 52 rhyming lines

Take sodium the explosive,
Add chlorine, which is erosive,
Then nourishing salt of the earth
By synthesis is given birth.
    Take two and make yourself a whole.
    Homogenize can be a goal.
    Dichotomy can merge to one.
    To separate can not be fun.
Think heads and tails as just one coin.
Just learn to integrate and join.
This age of new hybridity
Is a new singularity.
    Connect all civilization
    With synthesis and with fusion.
    Computers are unitary,
    Because of their code binary.
We're interconnected by jet,
And, also, by the internet.
Psychosomatic unites two.
Philanthropy can unite, too.
    Let's reconcile duality,
    And merge all of diversity.
    I tend to think evolution
    Unites all blocs as solution.
Have hybrid, multinational,
Integral, multicultural,
Holistic, and multiracial,
Interfaith, international,

Amalgamation, and global
Interdependence over all.
Change disparate into a blend.
Let's dissolve walls and make them end.
The wall between two cells may be
Knocked on to give signals, you see.
Communication's then a link.
Three comes out of two, don't you think?
  Just like two poles make one magnet.
  Ride two wheels and balance you'll get.
  Each knife edge has a left and right.
  Relaxing beats both fight and fright.
Condenser and current give charge.
These trinities don't disparage.
The lesson from all this to learn
Is that from two a "child" is born
  Take what is best out of our past.
  Don't waste it 'cause it needs to last.
  Take what's useful for the future;
  Apply it for our present cure.
All poets, writers and artists
Know there is need for two contrasts.
There's also need for unity.
This poet knows that, certainly.

Duality Has Two Sides
Feel The Pendulum's Pull

(Written in a meter of ..-..-..-..-)
Anapest Tetrameter
12 syllables in 60 alternately rhyming lines

Every life seems more troubles than comfort, we know.
But avoiding of troubles avoids part of life.
That avoidance can make you a Vincent Van Gogh,
Who had need to cut off his own ear with a knife.
    Now, the symbol of him cutting off of his ear
    Meant he didn't want even to hear himself think,
    Or to notice some pain that might be very near
    It showed loss of himself was right there on the brink.
If this happens to you, you won't own what's yourself,
And you'll spin out some tales to avoid being real.
Then you'll flip through your album that's there on your shelf
Like it's not even yours, and it's not a big deal.
    And you'll flip through this album like artists paintings;
    Feeling nothing that's there does belong just to you.
    When besieged by your life's acute painful feelings,
    You'll be feeling put down and you'll be feeling blue.
It's right then that your album should start to open
On identity and what shows you belonging.
For your family's love and their help will often
Pull you through until you will again be smiling.
    Prophet Daniel in the Bible, he predicts
    That the people in end times will run to-and-fro.
    When each circumstance of pain for you interdicts,
    Stop right then; start to pray to God who loves you so.
Don't get caught by vertiginous life and its whirl,
Or get lost and distracted within a daydream.
And don't let your defenses at that time unfurl,
When your life is more painful than you even deem.

Try your best to avoid seeing certain movies,
The ones which run from God, and are a form of *flight*.
Movies show our defenses to us in series
There are horror movies that are just full of *fright*.
Others show mythic plots that we call *falsity,*
With some vampires, or wolf man, or even wizards,
Or a Frankenstein, or a living-dead city.
And there's *fight* with its action-adventure hazards,
    Or escapism's comedy-like type of *fun.*
    If you see these you'll find you're not facing troubles,
    But you're using this entertainment just as one
    Blind defense to escape, while your stress all doubles.
Do you know the last time that real art made you cry,
Or feel closer to God, or made you start to think?
Did it change your down mood, and let you want to try?
There's ideals to which all of high art gives us link.
    All your life you should feel that you're fully alive.
    We should make of our lives a loving masterpiece.
    That's the goal to aim for and to constantly strive.
    And we'll all be much better for that, so don't cease.
Truly great art has now seemingly been replaced
By some art that's termed secular and not sacred.
And the fact that all pendulums swing must be faced,
As you feel each side pull you both now and ahead.
    But we dimly, also, remember perfection
    Within something that feels like a paradise lost.
    There was something there worth all of our attention,
    That gave a money's worth that was worth all the cost.
Now, no matter how life can hurt me 'til I wince,
The solution I feel for me may not be quick,
'Cause I feel that I am really an exiled prince.
But I, also, am, "Lord, the one you love is sick."

See And Say
The Urge To Be Heard

(Written in a meter of .-.-.-.-)
Iambic Tetrameter
8 syllables in 36 rhyming lines

Creative art, it seems to me,
Shows what the inner eyes can see.
Then when what's seen has had its say,
That true art shows God's face some way.
    Creative Spirit shows us love,
    Goodness, and wisdom from above.
    Examined life is worth living.
    Seek love, giving and forgiving.
Each artist wants to feel alive,
With heart full of love that will thrive.
And mind full of much truth to spare,
While spirit shows God's face with care.
    Defenses and our spirit make
    The life we live, or it's a fake.
    Duality with synthesis
    Gives trinity new emphasis.
Let's move beyond duality
To synthesize some trinity.
Then, reach higher transformation
With values and ideals' vision.
    Books show these things for us to see
    To help us toward our destiny.
    Poetic words show truth so clear
    That love and goodness too appear.
Whatever art you want to do,
Some urge you feel will help you through.
Use inner and use outer eyes.
Tell us of what gives you surprise.

Art starts with that creative urge
To be heard, but this may not merge
With your acceptance by us all.
All art does not hang on a wall.
Your life of self-sacrifice may
Not leave much art, just things to say
About life as a masterpiece,
Which shows us love that cannot cease.

Haunted By Restlessness
Catching God's Spark

(Written in a meter of .-.-.-.-)
Iambic Tetrameter
8 syllables in 32 rhyming lines

I don't think that we all are meant
To be peaceful in the present,
Because haunting is the intent
Of all forgotten resentment.
    The past and future join as plus
    Inside our present to haunt us.
    We all have wounds that never healed,
    And restlessness inside us sealed.
We've nostalgia that feels so raw,
Loves lost and found, and what we saw.
The present clings to what once was.
Our future does the same, because
    We cling with real anxiety
    To what has been and what will be.
    The present, too, has poor health threat.
    You'll feel its retributions, yet.
The present has its obsessions,
And heartaches, headaches, and passions.
St. Augustine named all of this.
He named it so we just can't miss.
    He called it a heart's restlessness,
    Which makes us stop and just confess,
    "Only in God can our hearts rest."
    Hearts only can rest in what's best.
God's in your solitude within,
From that experience you'll win.
You'll find inside any torment
This urge toward God, which will foment.

This Plato's "madness of the gods,"
It constantly beckons and nods,
To bring us to light from the dark.
Illumination has God's spark.

Truth
There's Lots Of It

(Written in a meter of .-.-.-.-)
Iambic Tetrameter
8 syllables in 24 rhyming lines

There's truth found in analogy,
And symbolism, simile.
The truth is not incognito
In slogan, maxim and motto.
    And truth is found in many quotes,
    Whose joy and wisdom "lifts all boats."
    Truth or opinion, they do meet
    In aphorisms, short and sweet.
A truism does not need proof.
Its truth goes simply "through the roof."
All sayings and all parables
Have truth that can "turn the tables."
    Wise axioms, remarks and such,
    With metaphors can teach us much.
    Touch hearts and souls with anecdotes.
    Move minds with "mental hugs" of quotes.
Greek sculpture has its ideal truth,
Loveable and tangible, both.
Wise sayings show that masterpiece,
Where truth, love and goodness increase.
    Truth is expressed in many ways.
    It's found in what each of us says.
    We never could ask a question
    If truth were not here for certain

God Is An Artist
Understanding Suffering

(Written in a meter of .-.-.-)
Iambic Pentameter
10 syllables in 24 rhyming lines

Infinite heat should stop all cold, we're told.
Should not infinite good stop evil cold?
To understand life's evil suffering,
Just think of God as artist creating.
    Art needs some light and dark, good and evil.
    So God allows that there is a devil.
    We only get to see a tiny part
    In our lifetime of God's creative art.
His art fills all of time and all of space.
To understand it's hard without God's grace,
For evil is a lack that God allows.
You don't create lack, 'cause it just follows.
    In a sense, illness is a lack of health,
    And poverty is just a lack of wealth.
    Job questioned God about life's suffering,
    And God asked Job if he saw things starting.
Job knew that God was then in charge, always,
For Job did not see God's creative days.
And God, like artists, He has to suffer
Creating His great works like none other.
    God is an artist doing what He wants.
    He covers each square inch, allowing grunts.
    But His benevolence is always there.
    The beauty is that God is always fair.

The Nutcracker
Christmas Ballet

(Written in a meter of .-.-.-.)
Iambic Tetrameter
8 syllables in 32 rhyming lines

I went to see the Nutcracker,
Which I do every November.
A lovely Christmas-time ballet,
It is a classic its own way.
    The basic thing there is to know
    Is that the cast within the show
    Consists of a whole ballet school.
    They are all ages, which is cool.
The music has worldwide renown.
Its plot is also widely known
About a family at Christmas,
Revolving around a young miss.
    Her nutcracker toy comes to life
    To help eliminate her strife.
    He helps her grow beyond her years
    By facing and conquering fears.
The various ballet dance scenes,
Based on the use of a child's dreams,
Combine with choreography
To give something worthwhile to see.
    What's also special just for me
    Is when a relative can be
    In the show that each year I see,
    Advancing in their roles yearly.
At times it's not a relative,
But a neighbor from where I live,
Or just someone that I might know.
No matter who, it adds some glow.

There's nothing better, we are told,
Than family unity of old,
With Christmas nostalgia unfurled.
This love can radiate the world.

Ride The Flow
A Lot Of Rhyme To Take

(Written in a meter of .-.-.-.-)
Iambic Tetrameter
8 syllables in 24 rhyming lines

What's in my poems that you like?
Can you ride their flow like a bike,
And feel known like the peak named Pike,
Or like the General named Ike?
 I want my poems to out psyche,
 And have a thrill, like tyke on trike.
 At least a rider who's named Mike,
 Using the turnpike to the dike.
Maybe I'll end up at the lake.
This is a lot of rhyme to take.
It hits you like an earthquake's quake,
But read on more, please, for my sake.
 I know you'll feel, if you partake,
 That you'll be free of every ache,
 'Cause my words are heartfelt, not fake.
 Right now, let's bake a cake for Jake.
Don't be left in this poem's wake,
There still are words that we can take.
For instance there's the word of "rake,"
Which will rhyme with the word, "snowflake."
 Why not change this rhyme overall,
 And have ourselves a rhyming ball?
 Let's start with gall, call, fall, and hall,
 And add in all, Gaul, tall, wall, mall.

It
Making Use Of It

(Written in a meter of .-.-.-.-)
Iambic Tetrameter
8 syllables in 28 rhyming lines

This is a poem about "it."
And it goes without saying it
That I'm always amazed by it.
And you'll be wanting more of it.
    Just think what you can do with it.
    People always talk about it.
    But first of all you must get it.
    We all want to have some of it.
And what would we do without it?
Every poem seems to have it.
Show me a poem without it.
Success is: "I think you've got it!"
    You may think this is full of it.
    Perhaps it is, 'cause I like it.
    The big question is, "What is it?"
    It is two letters we call "it.."
"Short and sweet" is what's said of it.
It fits right in, just all of it.
In truth, we can't do without it.
Power's in every bit of it.
    You have to give credit to it.
    In time we all consider it.
    And why didn't I think of it?
    Don't forget it, don't you let it.
I'll end this poem using it.
There would be no rhyme without it.
Its done it, and that's about it.
That sums it up; that's all of it.

That
Not This, But That

(Written in a meter of .-.-.-.-)
Iambic Tetrameter
8 syllables in 28 rhyming lines

This poem's all about just "that."
It's not about "this," only "that."
For what's remote, please do say, "that."
Oh that you'd make good use of that!
    You designate by saying, "that."
    A person or thing there is "that."
    If something's mentioned, then, that's "that."
    Contrast, when used, your "that" shows that.
We say, "Keep this; discard all that."
But don't you think we should keep "that."
You can't say "this" without some "that."
And that's a fact. Yes, it is that.
    Whatever we imply is "that,"
    And what we understand, that's "that."
    Extending goes as far as "that,"
    At least to the extent of "that."
Distinguish, please, your "this" from "that."
Unstressed in poems is this "that."
This poem doesn't show us that.
So now, what do you think of "that"?
    Go down the alphabet to "that."
    You'll pass by "bat" to get to "that."
    And also, "cat" right after that.
    Then "mat, pat, rat, sat," and then "that."
Can you think of a poem that
Has used so much of the word "that"?
I can't even imagine that.
This poem ends, so that is that.

Plots
Not A Submarine

(Written in a meter of .-.-.-.-)
Iambic Tetrameter
8 syllables in 28 rhyming lines

These are some plots I'm thinking of:
A boy meets girl; they fall in love.
They both hold hands, and start to kiss
With kisses that seem full of bliss.
    This classic plot it cannot miss.
    My other plots, they go like this:
    A predator goes seeking prey
    Or martyr comes who knows to pray.
Some disaster could happen here
Or funny thing to give us cheer.
A criminal can start to run
Or cowboy load to shoot his gun.
    My sleuths will solve for us each crime,
    While scientists will outwit time.
    These plots continue down the line.
    What they've in common is they're mine.
My soldiers march on, keeping stride,
To stop those who would rule worldwide.
I'll have skaters who sometimes fall,
And sports figures right on the ball.
    But the plot that is still the best
    Is the one passing every test.
    It's not a submarine in dives,
    But finding love that changes lives,
By finding someone very dear
To live life with, and very near.
This kind of love it drives out fear,
And wins an Oscar every year.

That Comes Before It
That's Not It

(Written in a meter of .-.-.-.-)
Iambic Tetrameter
8 syllables in 32 rhyming lines.

There once was a poem called "It."
A prior poem was called "That."
Most folks asked, "When did you write 'It'?"
The poet said, "Right after 'That'."
    Folks then would ask, "Right after what?"
    He'd say, "Not after 'What.' but 'That'."
    Confusion reigned, I'll tell you what.
    There was a mix-up over "That."
"It's not 'What' I've written," he'd say.
"It's 'It' and just 'That,' that I wrote."
"When did you do that?" they would say.
"Before 'It,' came 'That,' which I wrote."
    "But, *what* are you talking about?"
    Folks asked in confusion and doubt.
    "It's not 'What' I'm talking about.
    I've done 'That' without any doubt.
What comes before 'It' is just 'That.'
The time of my writing is clear."
But folks did not understand that,
And asked again their question clear.
    "When did you write 'It?' Please reply!
    That is just what we want to know."
    He said, "'That' is now my reply,
    'Cause 'That' is what you need to know.
There's no 'What,' just 'That,' and that's it.
That's all you need know about 'That.'
And all of 'That' comes before 'It.'
This answer, I hope, settles that."

One last question they asked of him:
"Is there more that you can tell us?"
And this is the answer from him:
" 'That's' not 'It,' and 'What's' not for us."

The potential of language
Truth, Justice and Change

(Written in a meter of .-.-.-.-)
Iambic Tetrameter
8 syllables in 32 lines of Free Verse

Please tell me what you think it takes
An astute seasoned journalist
To chronicle humanity,
As a human rights advocate,
    Extraordinary thinker,
    Major newspaper columnist,
    And a Pulitzer Prize winner,
    World traveler through Africa,
India, China, South Asia,
And the countries found in Europe,
To bring compassionate insights
Exposing the world's poverty,
    Global health, or earth's genocide.
    It takes a communicator
    Willing to set an agenda,
    And bring in front of the public
Neglected issues, so they will
Get attention and resources,
All directed to these problems,
Because communication and
    Scholarly investigation
    Create what causes social change.
    Human condition's heart always
    Resides in the use of language.
Great potential bursts forth out of
Ideas, and education,
And a country's moral fiber.
Communication brings about

Social justice and needed change.
Not only change of what is wrong,
But change of what countries do right,
For it's the truth that sets us free.

Big Words
Pretentious

(Written in a meter of ..-..-..-)
Anapest Trimeter
9 syllables in 40 rhyming lines

We all might call it fortuitous,
When words by accident come to us.
It's so propitious and auspicious,
Plus precocious and perspicacious.
   And all these big words are plenteous.
   They are enormous and marvelous;
   Also, delicious and prodigious.
   Use astute words and be generous.
But know, big words make me tremulous,
Because they are so monumentous.
They are so bounteous and precious.
Some are officious and outrageous.
   One fact I've learned that is tremendous:
   Bacteria are ubiquitous,
   Which means that they are found everywhere.
   They are copious and we should care.
Some science words seem quite courageous.
They speak of diseases contagious,
And speak with truth that's not mendacious.
Horrendous big words are atrocious.
   Another sentence that's capacious,
   And sounds bodacious and audacious:
   Ontogeny recapitulates
   Phylogeny. I like how that states.
Embryologic development
Just repeats evolution's intent.
Science uses the terms: vitreous,
Homogenous and homologous.

You won't find me being contentious,
As I use words that are momentous.
I'm loquacious and I'm ambitious,
But I'm not vicious or rebellious.
By now, my words may seem suspicious
That I'm trying to be malicious,
And very wicked and pernicious.
But I'm whimsical and capricious.
I'm felicitous and facetious;
Not avaricious or barbarous.
I'm not rapacious, felonious,
Nor perfidious, just pretentious.

Poetical Without Rhyme
Free Verse

(Written in a meter of .-.-.-)
Iambic Tetrameter
8 syllables in 36 lines of Free Verse

Real poets don't have to bother
To be poetical at all.
So too, all the real gardeners
Don't add perfume to the flowers.
    Most things occur naturally.
    I think that is the reason why
    We cherish free verse's magic
    Of ideas and emotions.
These free verse words take precedence
Without forcing them into rhyme.
Compare the magic called Santa,
Where, both, giving and family
    Take precedence over just him.
    The members of families have love
    That unites them in nostalgia,
    And Santa can't compete with that.
We remember from our childhood
All the warm feelings of Christmas.
These naturally take over,
Including faith in the unknown,
    And in something better to come.
    We tell kids about Santa Claus
    To help them grow up in a world
    That then is complete with magic,
Belief, and possibility.
We balance this against the shock
That our parents can sometimes lie,
Except about what's really true.

Above all this is: "Ho, ho, ho!"
The sound of joy and its laughter,
And all the feelings we call love,
Which children and adults treasure.
We celebrate these at birthdays.
And at the time of each Christmas,
Which is the birthday of Jesus.
You can't ask more from life than this.

The Sky At Night
Variegated Fascination

(Written in a meter of .-.-.-.-)
Iambic Tetrameter
8 syllables in 48 lines of Free Verse

Can anyone describe the sky
On nights so dark they're full of stars?
It's backlit perforation spots
Of shiny luminescent light.
> Like hot showers of punctate sparks
> That look like celestial fireworks.
> A silver dazzling large sparkler
> That burns intense and doesn't stop.

A giant's sweeping large black cloak
That's brightly mottled in the sky.
A shimmering garment that is
Full of fluorescent polka dots.
> All strewn in sprays of bright speckles.
> Like mirrored reflecting sequins,
> Or tiny scattered bright pinpoints
> Of sparkling, glowing, scattered light.

Just winking, and a twinkling;
Continuously flickering.
Like hot and shimmering spatters
Of yellow, white and also blue.
> A fleeing from some white hot forge
> With an explosive burst of glitz.
> I drink in this glistening sight
> Of scintillating glint that's there.

It's dappled, stippled and peppered
By dancing bright flashes that are
Like effervescent soda drinks
To satisfy a thirsty gaze.

Like light reflected on all walls
from mirrored, ceiling, dancehall balls.
Then suddenly there's the full moon,
A glowing, floating, golden disc.
It seems suspended by magic
To mesmerize and enchant me.
I cannot turn from these patterns
Of variegated splendor.
Such overwhelming bright glory!
When I close my eyes, I hurry
To open them again; not blink,
As all of this is sheer delight.
It's animated refreshment.
I don't want to miss anything,
Not one bit of revelation
Cast brilliantly before my eyes.
I only can thank God for this,
For it is there for me each night.
I only need to just look up
To gain each night's fascination.

Alliteration
Getting Out "D" Word

(Written in a meter of .-.-.-.-)
Iambic Tetrameter
10 syllables in 32 rhyming lines.

Depression and despair seem imminent
To those deployed to work in government.
Divided, distracted and deluded
That puts us in their group, we're included.
    Sometimes we're delighted or desirous,
    Or demanding until delirious.
    But many things occur, as you will see,
    While we experience what we can be.
Sometimes we're delicate or delicious,
Or even definitely dangerous.
But if we really want to be quite fair,
We will define with details what we share.
    And often we'll dictate and not debate,
    If desolate or quick to delegate.
    Don't decide to deride or to delete,
    You'll only get despondent from defeat.
In desperation we stay dependent,
Or act quite difficult and different.
Act dominant to defend what you say,
But don't use it as defense to delay.
    Some daring drug abuse may help dissolve
    Democracy that depends on resolve.
    Dilemma helps to make some folks digress,
    Who are not dying to digest distress.
Duplicity's deceit brings on duress.
Dramatic drama will maintain that mess.
At times we drink in dreamy loud droning.
A dreadful drawback seems to be brewing.

38

We have to douse what's dour, and what has doubt.
A drawing down is not what we're about.
We're not designed to be desultory.
What is destructive won't be our story.

Family gathering at my 80th Birthday Party

Grandchildren Outside The Museum

Science

Diamonds
What's Better

(Written in a meter of .-.-.-.-)
Iambic Tetrameter
8 syllables in 40 rhyming lines

For diamonds I'm searching this time
In pits, out of which I must climb.
Rough diamonds found right at the mine
Show glassy or translucent shine.
    They've facets and luster that's fine.
    Earth dug in buckets pulled by line
    Is screened and washed and inspected,
    For diamonds are what's expected.
But dull alluvial crystals
Are found in distant stream gravels.
In India these first were found
In gravel, and not in the ground.
    That was two thousand years ago.
    Since then they're found, I think you know,
    In Brazil and South Africa,
    And, also, now Australia.
Some twenty countries now produce
All diamonds for world's market use.
Some topaz water worn pebbles,
Mimics diamond it resembles.
    Specific gravities both seem
    Close to similar, hence the dream
    Of a "diamond celebration."
    Each gem found gives this reaction.
Now, diamond is derived, I've heard,
From *adamas*, an old Greek word.
It means "unconquerable," that's true,
'Cause its hardness cuts all in view.

Pure diamond, carbon's crystal form,
Cuts all minerals; they'll conform.
But it shatters by hammer blow,
And that is a good thing to know.
What's harder that diamond is this:
A true love that's sealed with a kiss.
Unconquerable love is vast.
It may seem soft, but it will last.
Immortal love will never end.
Like diamond, it's a girl's best friend.
It's better, 'cause love's everywhere,
And something that we all can share.

Fool's Gold
Gold Fever

(Written in a meter of .-.-.-.-)
Iambic Tetrameter
8 syllables in 36 rhyming lines

I want some gold, the element,
Then I'll be rich, that's my intent.
To do that I'll need in my fold
Detective Sherlock Holmes of old.
  'Cause finding elements, like gold,
  Is elementary, I'm told.
  But finding gold takes more than brains.
  It's hard work, which requires pains.
I'll have to get up off my rear,
And work real hard, at least a year.
I failed to take into account
That Fool's Gold is in great amount.
  There's more of that than Gold, I hear.
  Attached to each a fool seems near.
  I was among their ranks 'til now,
  When gold fever left me somehow.
Those with gold shouldn't make bad rules,
Which, when enforced, make them look fools.
Don't set aside the Golden Rule,
Or just yourself is who you'll fool.
  We all should do unto others,
  Since we are truly all brothers,
  As we would like done unto us.
  That means to share, not crave surplus.
I let surplus become my creed,
Because I am so full of greed,
Expecting more than what I need.
That leads to war, where all can bleed.

World hunger's now in the docket,
In part from what's in my pocket.
If charities begin to fail,
Hold tight to the nearest handrail.
True value isn't found in gold,
But in the love your heart can hold.
Away from gold your mind must switch,
If you want to be really rich.

Anatomy
A Privilege

(Written in a meter of .-.-.-.-)
Iambic Tetrameter
8 syllables in 36 rhyming lines

Anatomy is dissection
That exposes for inspection.
Organs and structures are laid bare;
You separate them all with care.
    Dissect the word "anatomy."
    It means "without cutting," you see.
    And it's a very old fine art.
    Each medical student takes part.
You do not start off with the head.
It's covered up; you start instead
Your first cut at the front of chest.
A Y-shape from shoulders is best.
    As cuts meet you continue down.
    Cut too deep and professors frown.
    As you memorize and you learn,
    There is much midnight oil to burn.
The nerves that come out from the spine,
When they meet at the skin they're fine.
Blood vessels can be tied with thread.
Not having a clean field you dread.
    The body's studied in sections,
    And you're given the directions.
    After the head and neck you're told,
    "It's now all downhill," but that's old.
As medical students dissect,
They treat all bodies with respect.
This chance to learn that they're given
Makes them grateful; keeps them driven.

All doctors need anatomy,
No matter what their specialty.
You can't learn it all from a book,
Because you have to cut and look.
We're thankful for the privilege.
And this seems like an old adage:
If you bequeath your dead body,
Your gift will help save somebody.

Neutrinos
Ghost Particles

(Written in a meter of .-.-.-.-)
Iambic Tetrameter
8 syllables in 52 rhyming lines

Neutrinos go through steel items
Like comets through solar systems.
To our touch steel may feel solid,
But inside steel there's much space hid.
    Neutrinos seem a miracle,
    A subatomic particle.
    They do not have electric charge,
    So there is nothing to discharge.
Electric or magnetic force
Can't capture them at all, of course.
These particles they are neutral.
They're numerous and multiple.
    Some trillions pass, and make no bond,
    Through our bodies every second.
    They go through earth near speed of light,
    And move through us both day and night.
They come out from the Big Bang, plus,
Exploding stars and sun to us.
Ghost particles, a physicist
Called them; a term we can't resist.
    It's correct for us to infer
    Neutrino release can occur
    From supernovas, if you please,
    And from colliding galaxies.
Atoms, before and after they
Have radioactive decay,
Will have records made of their mass
To gauge neutrino's mass to pass.

Spectrometers can do this task,
And that is not too much to ask.
All scientists like to measure,
For measuring gives them pleasure.
Two dozen or so particles
Make subatomic articles.
Among the lightest of these are
Neutrinos, of those found so far.
Cosmic rays have outer space birth,
But they can't penetrate the earth.
Neutrinos can, plus, switch with ease
Three different identities.
Physicists say they oscillate
Among three "flavors," which is great.
Flavor to oscillate takes mass;
Anti-neutrinos can't surpass.
When measuring neutrinos we
Measure one flavor, don't you see,
The collision for electron.
The other two we'll work upon.
Neutrino research can be found
In many places underground.
Research goes on throughout the world
To get particle facts unfurled.

Mathematics
Many Branches

(Written in a meter of .-.-.-.-)
Iambic Tetrameter
8 syllables in 40 rhyming lines

All lovers of mathematics,
They like to use some statistics.
And measure with meter metrics
Or calculate our genetics.
    There's more to it, you will agree,
    'Cause numbers reach infinity.
    There's also Relativity,
    And also Probability.
You start with simple addition,
Then move on to some subtraction.
Next thing, you are multiplying,
And moving on to dividing.
    Soon, fractions and Geometry,
    Algebra, Trigonometry,
    Calculus, and Topology;
    Number sequence Fibonacci.
You may be thinking this depicts
A group to call, "numbers addicts,"
Who delve in zero, pi, and more,
And who calculate what's the score.
    And who solve Fermat's last theorem;
    Poincare's conjecture problem,
    And leave only one thing unsolved.
    Prime numbers here can be involved.
It's the Riemann hypothesis,
Which is worth some analysis,
Because the Clay Math. Institute
Has a reward for those astute.

So join in with computer codes,
Graphs, sets, groups, and fractal's abodes.
Immerse yourself in matrices
And mathematics practices.
Square roots, also numerators,
Axes and denominators,
Square numbers, also integers,
These terms help us to use numbers.
Axioms and theorems persist,
Even coordinates exist.
Postulates and distributions,
All these help mathematicians.

Minimally Invasive Surgery
VATS

(Written in a meter of .-.-.-.-.-)
Iambic Pentameter
10 syllables in 36 rhyming lines

Video-assisted thorascopic
Surgery or VATS is a new topic.
"Port-accessed" and "video-assisted"
Are terms that you'll see frequently listed.
 Minimally invasive surgery
 Uses vast progress in technology,
 Namely, thorascopic endoscopy,
 Robotics, and small thoracotomy.
Plus, bipolar radiofrequency
With some focused ultrasonography
Of high intensity for ablation
Treatment of atrial fibrillation.
 You'll hear other terms: cryoablation,
 3-dimension visualization,
 Off pump, cardioplegia, lesion,
 Also, autonomic denervation.
There will be pacemaker implantation,
Normal sinus rhythm restoration,
Partial sternotomy operation,
And, also, silicone-band occlusion.
 Be aware of ganglionic mapping.
 Please do not let these terms find you napping.
 Some terms that you'll hear used are: microwave
 And laser, 'cause they help some lives to save.
And furthermore, what may need to be done:
Left atrial appendage exclusion.
Polyester fabric is used like slips
To cover some epicardial clips.

And patients with a history of stroke
Cause some worry, because stroke is no joke.
Operation time and the length of stay
Are recorded to help find the best way.
A specialized navigation device
With robot-assistance can help suffice
To have mini-invasive surgery
Become widespread, and not a luxury.

Sand
Arenology

(Written in a meter of .-.-.-.-)
Iambic Tetrameter
8 syllables in 56 rhyming lines

Arenology is study
Of sand; not land that is muddy.
Arenosus means, in Latin,
Sandy or gritty, not satin.
    Psammophiles is another word
    For those who study sand, I've heard.
    Psammos is Greek, I understand.
    It, also, does translate as "sand."
Collectors are Arenophiles,
And, also, they are Psammophiles.
Dunes are sand that's blown into piles.
What's collectable goes for miles.
    Aeolean deposits are
    The wind blown dunes, which can move far.
    Streams, dunes, sand banks, spits and beaches
    Are within collector's reaches.
Some glacial outwash dunes are found
From sand deposits from that ground.
White Sands, New Mexico, we know,
Has a gypsum sand dune field flow.
    A large dune field is called an "erg."
    Do not confuse that with "iceberg."
    Dry inland former lake or sea
    Gives large complex dunes that we see.
A dune's shape can be concentric,
Linear, or parabolic,
Or longitudinal looking,
And even sometimes reversing.

The trough between dunes is called "slack."
Dune's shorter leeward side, or back,
Or "slip face" gets slowly advanced.
The larger windward side gets pushed.
Recently weathered granite and
Gneiss make angular quartz "sharp sand"
Or "grus" used for making concrete.
Particles in sand are discrete.
 A high silica sandstone site
 In East Missouri is just right
 To give Crystal City its name,
 'Cause the sand makes glass, hence that fame.
Above low tide limit we see
Coastal deposits and debris.
A "storm beach" has crests of old berms.
More inland is where a dune forms.
 Dunes are formed as the wind blows sand,
 Which then accumulates inland.
 Each hourglass holds sands of time,
 Which we can't stop, even with rhyme.
The beach, we call it the "shore zone."
Collectors there are not alone.
For we can't help it, we love sand.
It seems to flow right through our hand.
 The sand feels good between our toes.
 And makes sand castles, each child knows.
 A great experience to reach
 Is someday to go to the beach.

Reboot For Mood Upgrade
Technology

(Written in a meter of .-.-.-.-)
Iambic Tetrameter
8 syllables in 40 rhyming lines

Technology for kings and queens
Gave all of us computer screens.
Each came with a keyboard and mouse
To bring great changes to our house.
    And big screens for TV came too,
    'Cause that's the size we like to view.
    Then came a phone complete with app.,
    That can plug into a laptop.
Add wireless and remote control,
For costs to put you in a hole.
You'll still buy downloads and upgrades,
The latest games and study aids.
    We've learned about: the web worldwide,
    Where chips and wires can all get "fried,"
    Dos, input, output, and icons,
    And phone internet connections.
There's notebooks now that are readers,
And microphones with their speakers;
Hand-held tablets with libraries,
And rechargeable batteries.
    Both analog and digital
    Seem to be where it's pivotal.
    I think most folks may now have seen
    A split or dual color screen.
These are no longer debated:
Voice and motion activated;
Save programs for later viewing;
Software and hardware upgrading.

We've screens in cars and eye-glasses,
With new things as each year passes.
And everything's getting combined;
Mobile capacity's in mind.
I've heard there's a computer suit.
I wonder how it does reboot?
This suit that is electrified
Must have a firewall deep inside.
What has our technology done?
Our lives are still not full of fun.
For something higher we're all made.
Poets can help our *lives* upgrade.

Stem Cells
Help May Cause Harm

(Written in a meter of .-.-.-.-)
Iambic Tetrameter
8 syllable in 28 lines of Free Verse

Our pluripotent stem-cells come
With an unique capacity
That's an amazing thing to see.
These cells can change or morph into
    Some other types of living cells.
    This potential is used, of course,
    To replace some living tissues,
    And be for us another source.
We find these cells in embryos,
And also in some adult cells,
Which in adults must be induced
To return to embryo state.
    Both lines of cells have big problems
    Of duplications in genome
    Or deletions in the genome.
    We know that cancer may come from
Genetic abnormalities.
Despite this, these cells we implant
To treat spinal cord injury;
Macular degeneration.
    And even though help may cause harm,
    The patients want to walk or see.
    That's how it is with all that's new,
    It may save or it might kill you.
What else can all the doctors do,
But proceed very carefully,
And also quite ethically?
We pray it goes successfully.

Three Things Can Relate
Physics Theory

(Written in a meter of .-.-.-.-.-)
Iambic Pentameter
10 syllables in 100 rhyming lines

Three systems that are called Biology,
And, also, Culture and Technology,
They follow three rules called evolution,
Which has inheritance, variation,
    Plus, what can rule out chance called selection.
    A rule of three may extend to ion.
    So let's look at Physics to find some three.
    And when we look it's there, most certainly.
Cyclotron tracks look straight, loop or spiral.
Trinity, triad or three seems vital.
Elemental fermions group in three
Generations, with six quarks named, plainly.
    Postulated point-like particles are
    Preons, parts of quarks and leptons, so far.
    And preons act like ribbons, as they twist
    Left, right, or not, as each one will insist.
Various braids give us, In a nutshell,
Unlike particles of standard model.
Another triple fact that's not too old:
Three quarks make protons and neutrons, we're told.
    Please note, each flavor of quark comes in three
    Colors according to the QCD.
    That's short for quantumchromodynamics.
    Three things can relate for many topics.
When three preons are braided together
Emergent state particles will occur,
Because of different ways to make a braid,
And knot the edges of the graph that's made.

Let's call these: coherent excitations;
Causal dynamic triangulations.
Conceptual language gives unity
To Quantum theory/Relativity.
When there's collision between particles,
Between them and their antiparticles,
They both annihilate to bring upon
The scene a triad from released "photon."
    An antiparticle called positron
    Meets electron to give us two photon.
    Three forces are photons, bosons, gluons.
    The weak force corresponds to weak bosons.
Just cut one of three Borromean Rings,
The rings will fall apart as separate things.
But three Hopf rings, they are so interlocked,
You cut one and two will remain still locked.
    Compare these rings to atom's orbitals,
    Although comparison has its pitfalls.
    Some crystals form in different shapes, of course,
    Because these crystals may be trimorphorous.
The Periodic Table got its hint
To form from the Law of Triads blueprint,
Where the second element out of three
Averaged between the first and third, you see.
    There is such a thing as entangled state.
    Two or three particles share in that fate.
    And parents and child share in that state too.
    All nature seems to have a triple view.
Ernest Rutherford used words in his day,
Like alpha, beta, or gamma decay.
These were for radioactivity,
And for its emission activity.
    Radioactive nuclides come from three
    Natural sources to us all, namely,
    Radiogenic and primordial
    And cosmogenic nuclides for us all.

A neutron decays through beta decay
To form into one proton that will stay.
Two fragments from the nucleus will leave.
One's a neutrino that we don't retrieve.
    The other makes for a third article,
    An electron called beta particle.
    Space, time and matter they seem to persist.
    And theories to void them they do exist.
We're used to having space, time and matter,
Along with land, sea and air, which occur
To show us all solid, liquid and gas.
Please note all of this three, don't let it pass.
    An alpha decay ejects two protons
    Of alpha particle with two neutrons.
    This helium atom loss brings balance.
    What's excess is shed to stop imbalance.
Particles or energy can increase.
Gamma ray is an energy release.
It is a highly energized photon.
Cosmic rays seems to be, in main, proton,
    Lose three in radioactive decay:
    A beta particle, and gamma ray,
    And antineutrino; you'll supervene
    Carbon-14 to nitrogen-14.
A particle has mass and some motion,
Which moves it in a certain direction.
Its mass takes a position out in space.
And speed of momentum changes that place.
    A wave has wavelength, amplitude and phase
    That may act in ribbon, tube or string ways.
    All three may connect in loop, braid or twist.
    A focus on three seems to just persist.
Note that electron, proton and neutron,
They form all the atoms we think upon.
Our world of quanta seems three dimension.
Relation of triples needs attention.

Quantum Dimensions
Trying To Keep Count

(Written in a meter of .-.-.-.-)
Iambic Tetrameter
8 syllables in 36 rhyming lines

We're used to our three dimensions.
They're real, and they're not inventions.
We name them width and depth and height.
Perspective we call depth of sight.
    Add time to bring the score to four.
    Beside these four let's add some more:
    There's symmetry of particles,
    They all have antiparticles.
This balances electric charge.
What's neutral then can yet discharge.
Atomic particles behave
As quantum packages or wave.
    So wavelength, frequency, or speed,
    And amplitude and phase we need.
    There's left and right, and back and forth;
    Spin up and down that's not from North.
Topology and rotation
Are used for orientation.
Don't forget there's orbits and shells
With inner and outer levels.
    Outer shells give to us valence;
    Everything stays in a balance.
    There's also color and flavor.
    Entanglement we can't ignore.
It's found in pairs or trinity.
There's Heisenberg Uncertainty,
Plus, Borromean and Hopf Rings,
And multiverses, branes and strings.

It all has such nice symmetry.
There's even supersymmetry.
Such theory flexibility
Makes for great possibility.
Dimension includes many things,
And not just quanta, waves and rings.
There's coherent excitations;
And causal triangulations.
There's also what's called background free,
Braids, loops, gauge field, infinity.
It makes for quite a big array
But that's how physics thinks today.

Tin, Gin & Uranium
Oh Brother!

(Written in a meter of ..-..-..-..-)
Anapest Tetrameter
12 syllables in 12 rhyming lines

What's the greatest idea, that has ever been?
Did it involve uranium, tin and some gin?
Someone had that idea once; they called it great,
To mix all of these up and to not hesitate.
    What they made was then called an atomic cocktail,
    Which they thought had a power that was without fail.
    But a very big problem showed up after all,
    When the storms rolled on by, and the rain drops did fall.
For you see, falling rain on the morning after,
Caused those who had imbibed to shout out, "Oh brother!"
For the rain hit the tin and the uranium,
And that shock made a loud noise in their cranium.

Computer Language
Old Words Have New Meanings

(Written in a meter of .-. .-. .-. .-)
Amphibrach Tetrameter
11 syllables in 20 rhyming lines

Computers, like pianos, have their *keyboards*,
But they are not used for the playing of chords.
Like people, computers can get *viruses*.
You don't call for doctors, just tech services.
    Computers, like houses, can have a *mouse pad*.
    Some mice live in one; the other's our new fad.
    Computers, like TV shows, have their *programs*,
    But their programs can send to you your exams.
Computers have *memory*; that's just like me.
But their *cursor* does not use profanity.
Computer *hard drives* don't involve any cars,
And so, when they *crash*, you don't wake seeing stars.
    Plus, their *CD's* do not belong in the bank.
    And *click* and to *point* never lowers your rank.
    Their *applications* don't get you employment.
    No spiders, just *webs,* are in development.
What's *floppy* refers only just to some discs
By now you can see there are many topics,
Where new meanings for old words now does exist.
This trend for the future is sure to persist.

Unintended Consequence
Collateral Damage

(Written in a meter of .-.-.-.-)
Iambic Tetrameter
8 syllables in 36 rhyming lines

All that we do that does make sense
Has unintended consequence.
There's increasing complexity,
Which seems like a necessity.
 An example is hybrid cars,
 Or sending missions off to Mars.
 Essential or just whimsical
 Creates effects that touch us all.
Collateral damage is us,
And that creates a lot of fuss.
For every cause expect effect.
Start out to do, and then expect.
 Life's kind of like a spreading wave;
 We hope that it will lift and save.
 But some are lifted, others harmed.
 And mostly everyone's alarmed.
Who can predict when bubbles burst,
Or just for what we all may thirst?
The tides of life may rise and fall,
But there's response, if you recall.
 Computational medicine
 Plans to help us, we imagine.
 Bioinformatics is new,
 And bioengineering, too.
Molecular biology,
Also, nano-technology,
Collaborate to give a start
To help us out, 'cause we are smart.

The lesson is: We keep alive
What's important; for it we'll strive.
And then we'll watch for "come what may,"
To see what forces come in play.
We can't predict too far ahead,
The unexpected comes instead.
Because of this don't stay in bed.
Life's not retreat, but something led.

Nothing
Zero

(written in a meter of .-.-.-.-)
Iambic Pentameter
10 syllables in 32 lines of Free Verse

If nothing is ventured then nothing's gained,
But nothing can come out of just nothing.
There's Ground Zero and there's Zero Hour,
But nothing doing is all null and void.
    How can there be something when it is not?
    But a zero is infinity's twin.
    Is all this much to do about nothing?
    For no one goes out to buy zero fish.
Why does a gaping nothing have a gape?
A vanishing point is just a nothing.
All of us use zero as a number,
And all we know is nothing about it.
    This seems to me just a big play on words.
    I feel like a cipher that's come to naught.
    Just look at what all of this talk has brought.
    It has brought all of us to just nothing.
Infinitesimally small is naught.
But not so small that we can neglect it.
Naught is so small that it can't be measured,
But of numbers it's the one most treasured.
    Lines and points are dual to each other.
    Imaginary numbers do exist.
    Don't think that zero has nothing to do.
    Its work is to explain its use to you.
When you are expecting to find something,
It affects you greatly to find nothing.
But how can nothing affect you greatly?
I guess it can when there's nothing to fear.

If only I could get to zero in
On the use of using empty numbers,
Then maybe I would start to feel at last
That I could say more now about nothing.

Pi
A Constant

(Written in a meter of .-.-.-.-.-)
Iambic Pentameter
10 syllables in 32 rhyming lines

A circle has a constant ratio
Of around and across, I think you know.
The circumference and diameter
Has a constant ratio everywhere.
    Dividing the circumference by its
    Diameter gives a number that fits.
    This constant number is what we call "pi;"
    Three point one four one five nine does apply.
All this was known two thousand years, B.C.,
When its exactness had no certainty.
The first to know were Babylonians,
And also to know were the Egyptians.
    We've learned that their old formulas don't lie,
    And that there's more to learn about this pi.
    Pi when multiplied by the radius
    Squared gives a circle's area to us.
By the end of the 16th century
Thirty decimal places correctly
Were known for pi, and 1844
Had two hundred places known, to give more.
    A computer was used to calculate
    Pi in 1949 on that date.
    Up to two thousand and thirty-seven
    Correct places became know to us then.
In 1967 pi was found
By computer to five hundred thousand.
Pi can't be a two number ratio.
It's an irrational number, you know.

The crumbs left by all giants are boulders.
We see far 'cause we stand on their shoulders.
Mathematics constantly advances.
It's also found in music and dances.

Quadrivium
Ancient Curriculum

(Written in a meter of .-.-.-.-)
Iambic Tetrameter
8 syllables in 20 rhyming lines

I've heard about Quadrivium.
It is ancient curriculum
Made up of the classical arts,
Which were divided in four parts.
    They started with arithmetic,
    Then geometry and music,
    And finally astronomy,
    Which was then called cosmology.
Liberal arts education
Did not have much history then.
Or science, law or other things
That modern school to us now brings.
    Yet what they knew then was so vast,
    Important and true, it did last.
    At the dawn of complexity
    They're there already, certainly.
There are things we should not forget,
For if we do we will regret.
Those things are: What's been found that's true,
And therefore should be taught to you.

Jewel thieves
Real Treasure

(Written in a meter of .-.-.-.-)
Iambic Tetrameter
8 syllables in 24 rhyming lines

Where there are jewels, you'll find thieves.
That's what each gem owner believes.
And so they safeguard their treasures
By taking all safety measures.
    They buy a safe and try to hide
    It's location, where it's inside.
    They keep their real jewels locked in,
    And wear fake jewels that's their twin.
And that is not all that they try,
For insurance is what they buy.
They try to cover any loss,
The likes of which would make them cross.
    When jewels that they own aren't worn,
    These owners are sad and forlorn
    Without gem dazzle on their side,
    And richness that fills them with pride.
They value what is their pleasure,
Which is to wear gems at leisure.
To steal that pride is like they've died.
That's why we may be on thieves' side.
    For we must all humble ourselves.
    Find that Bible truth for yourselves.
    Store your treasure up in Heaven,
    Away from jewel thieves, amen.

The text within the image reads:

SOME SAY HE IS EVIL
OTHERS INSIST THAT
HE IS NOBLE...
IN REALITY, HE IS NEITHER-
HE IS JUST A WOLF...
GOD MADE HIM FOR A
PURPOSE, AND THAT
PURPOSE HE SERVES.

"THE GRAY WOLF"
KCessna
2012

The Gray Wolf
Some say he is evil. Others insist that he is noble...In
reality, he is neither- He is just a wolf...God made him
for a purpose, and that purpose he serves.
(Art by artist Kit Cessna 2012)

Family Gathered At A North Carolina Museum

Love

Surgeons Display A Love That's Deep
Little Things Distract From Big

(Written in a meter of .-.-.-.-)
Iambic Tetrameter
8 syllables in 46 rhyming lines

Small things tie us up quite nicely.
That's Lilliputian strategy.
You notice pebbles in your shoe,
Before the big things facing you.
    David with just a little stone
    Could knock you out or make you groan.
    A superpower now must face
    Small crises all over the place.
An enemy makes us fearful.
We fall for that if not careful.
We are capable to swat flies
Or knock them out of our blue skies.
    But violence can't control life,
    It's love that conquers any strife.
    Surgeons display a love that's deep,
    Whenever they work while you sleep.
The poor folks who live in Haiti
Or Africa get helped and see
Physicians are to them as gold,
Or of more value we are told.
    From their volunteer's attitude
    They seek for pay just gratitude.
    Their helper is a nurse or nun.
    The tropic heat cannot be fun.
Be thankful surgeons are on call
To operate when you next fall.
Where you live, please, just hope and pray
A surgeon's there for you today.

Not one who thinks lifestyle schedules,
Or reimbursement types of rules,
But one, like most, dedicated.
Just hope that job's not vacated.
We need more surgeons, that's a fact,
But government is slow to act.
The crisis coming up real soon
Is not little or solved by June.

Secret Agent
One Unburnt Bridge

(Written in a meter of .-.-.-.-)
Iambic Tetrameter
8 syllables in 28 rhyming lines

Foreign countries with their pageants
Are where you'll find secret agents.
Who want to steal state documents,
And find out all new troop movements.
    I'm a secret agent in part,
    Because I want to steal your heart.
    I'll find the key to your heart's lock,
    For your love I hope to unlock.
Therefore, I follow every clue
In how to reach and interest you.
So be forewarned and stay on guard,
For falling in love isn't hard.
    Don't try to outwit what's your fate,
    For synchronicity's not late.
    Some hidden forces are around.
    When you find them, then you'll be found.
A secret agent has to learn
That there are some things you must burn.
I've burnt some bridges after me,
But one bridge stays eternally.
    Your connection of love to me,
    And my eternal love for thee.
    That is some real old bridge right there,
    Connecting us, because we care.
We stroll upon it hand in hand,
Now that you wear my wedding band.
I think it's fair to say right now,
"This secret agent has learned how."

Your Favorite
Ice Cream

(Written in a meter of .-.-.-.-)
Iambic Tetrameter
8 syllables in 20 rhyming lines

Please do for me a big favor.
Tell me your favorite flavor
Of ice-cream that you most savor.
I'll etch it upon a paver.
    Most folks, they say, scream for ice cream,
    But ice cream's just part of my dream.
    A dream that is to have my wife
    Cherish what is within her life.
I don't want to forget a thing
About you that means anything.
For my love for you is so great,
I'd gladly sell my whole estate
    To give you what you cherish most,
    If you'll just let me be your host
    To sponsor an ice-cream party,
    Where you can get to eat hearty.
For I would give the world to you,
Or the cosmos, if that would do,
To make you happier than now,
As we recite our wedding vow.

More Than Defenses
Love Is The Goal

(Written in a meter of .-.-.-.-)
Iambic Tetrameter
8 syllables in 36 rhyming lines

An animal out in the woods,
Or someone who protects their goods,
Confronted then, by a stranger,
Reacts to what may be danger.
    They have a choice to run away,
    Or stand and both start in to play.
    They also can freeze just from fright,
    Or even stand and have a fight.
Defense includes some falsity.
To save our life or property,
We will deny or falsify.
All the defenses we will try.
    No fight, or fright, or flight, or fun,
    Or falsity can beat a gun.
    There is another way to act.
    It's more loving, and that's a fact.
Let's start to do what Jesus said,
And love, forgive and give, instead.
We all are more than animal,
For humans are spiritual.
    Both qualities are in fusion,
    Like an optical illusion.
    At times they may seem separate.
    They've unity we can't forget.
When parts combine they make a whole.
Include and always count your soul.
For humans are much more than parts,
Because of love that's in their hearts.

Life's always paradox to us,
With opposites we all discuss.
And we must change to be constant.
The wise and happy they don't rant.
Whatever confronts you today,
And what it might make you to say,
Remember you've got heart and soul,
And love is what should be your goal.

Trouble in the Home
Who's To Blame?

(Written in a meter of .-.-.-.-)
Iambic Tetrameter
8 syllables in 28 rhyming lines

I'm angry with my wife today,
So I won't let her have her say.
I'll retreat to "silent treatment,"
Which lets us stew in resentment.
    Our children they don't understand,
    And I've no answers close at hand,
    So family anxiety
    Is there for everyone to see.
When stressed at work I seem to need
My wife to blame for any deed
That I consider ruffles me,
'Cause it does not support poor me.
    I'm under pressure and high stress,
    The kind that no one else can guess.
    When I need her the very most,
    She tends to treat me like a ghost.
We both should talk and sort things out.
But she'll make me feel like a lout.
Then I tend to belittle her;
We end up where we were before.
    You should not go to bed angry,
    That old rule was made just for me.
    There is room here for compromise,
    Which we should do if we are wise.
Our love and family need us
To settle this and stop our fuss.
I'm willing to make the first move.
My mood of anger I'll remove.

Surrounded by Love
Awareness

(Written in a meter of .-.-.-.-)
Iambic Tetrameter
8 syllables in 68 rhyming lines

A way to live is acceptance.
It's nature's way of existence.
It is a life that is expressed,
And not a life that is repressed.
    One only has to just take part;
    Aware of what is in your heart.
    You're part of life's reality,
    So be aware while you just be.
You don't have to push the river.
It flows, just like your love for her.
You can't jump in and change the course.
Relax or you'll just have remorse.
    Be like a child that's on the beach,
    Gather seashells, but please see each.
    Enjoy them all like they're diamonds.
    And cherish life and all its bonds.
Just disappear in existence.
Avoid going with indulgence.
And understand what does exist,
For love can touch stars through the mist.
    Silence is pregnant; words are dead,
    For they are language in your head.
    Thinking brings misunderstanding,
    And clouds of thoughts interpreting.
Feelings bring you outside of mind,
They're the silent love language kind,
Where each other's presence speaks much,
As much as does each other's touch.

Inexpressible love it shows.
It overflows, all of us knows.
We are mystery with powers.
We move like poets through flowers.
Don't throw out flowers; they have seed.
The seed for new flowers you'll need.
Seeds need soil, climate and bright sky,
To make more flowers that will die.

Ambitious seeds long for future,
To grow and flower is their lure.
Seeds cannot rest; seeds cannot sleep.
They reach the surface from the deep.
Seeds make flowers, and seeds make trees.
And seeds make humans, when we please.
Be sensitive, have emotion;
Both will bring communication.

It may seem strange, but it is true,
Seeing someone, out of the blue,
Looking ridiculous is when,
You find that you're in love right then.
Sentiments and vulnerable,
These both are really loveable.
You cannot laugh more than you need.
And one good laugh brings more to breed.

Change noisy clamor deep inside
To sweet harmony on your side.
Two arrows from two different bows
Will hit one target, each one knows.
Seek unity, not just union.
Joined is not the same as fusion.
One health can conquer all disease.
True love is more than just a tease.

By now you're asking this question,
"What is this poem's suggestion?"
In answer, to make this quite clear:
"Love is the answer to all fear.

We know what we experience,
And we feel, when we are not tense.
To know, we must become aware,
And love surrounds us everywhere"

Graduation
My Final One Is Near

(Written in a meter of .-.-.-.-)
Iambic Tetrameter
8 syllables in 36 rhyming lines

Our graduations always come,
And we will all have to face some.
Sometimes there can be long delay,
But other times it's now, today.
    Each one will bring some sad goodbye,
    With enough loss to make you cry.
    To graduate means moving on,
    And leaving some to think upon.
You wish your life could stop and stay,
But time moves things another way.
We all must go into the field
To find the treasure it can yield.
    You have to buy the field, you know,
    To own its treasure; reap and sow.
    A marriage is graduation
    In which you both get attention.
You both are grown and so mature
That you can plan your new future.
Life's not all moonlight and roses,
But daylight and dirty dishes.
    Each birth and milestone you can say
    Is graduation its own way.
    There's been a lot across the years.
    I hope that never disappears.
When you're old and "around the bend,"
Your graduations have their end.
For some that day comes all too soon,
Each time it leaves its mournful croon.

You can move on, and still not leave,
If you love someone and believe.
Promotion then is the notion
That fills us all with emotion.
I think my final time is near,
Which doesn't give me any fear,
Because of love for my dear wife.
She is my Heaven and my life.
Death means I'll be Above with her
And all I love, at God's order.
From what I've found here about love,
I'll gladly graduate Above.

Christmas Is A Birthday (1)
Christ is in Christmas (1)

(Written in a meter of .-..-..-.-)
Anapest Tetrameter
10 syllables in 36 rhyming lines

The night before Christmas is Christmas Eve.
And Christmas is when children all believe
In Santa Claus, who knows if they're naughty
Or nice enough for their gifts and party.
    More than gifts, there's faith, family and food,
    Which help us create what's the Christmas mood.
    I'm Santa's helper as a volunteer,
    Whose job it is to spread some Christmas cheer.
Don't misunderstand, cheer does not mean beer.
I try to remove loss of hope and fear.
I do that by reminding all who care
That Christmas means that you get gifts and share.
    The night before Christmas is Christmas Eve.
    For Christians that's when we look to receive
    The gift of Christ's birth in which we believe;
    Grateful that sin's guilt He came to relieve.
Christ tends to get lost in tinsel and lights.
His birth gets overlooked by stress and fights.
Except for those cherishing Silent Night,
Who keep Christ in Christmas as their delight.
    This time of the year gives us breaks from school,
    And great emphasis on the Golden Rule.
    We trim a tree and choose each ornament,
    But "love your God" is the first Commandment.
Don't worry about Santa or his sleigh.
Just try your best to pray and to obey.
For what is better than a Christmas card?
It's keeping Christ in Christmas; that's not hard.

After a meal we watch shows on TV,
Or we read books, or just talk pleasantly.
Remember to thank God for all His gifts,
Especially the gift of Christ who lifts.
We talk of reindeer Rudolph's red nose shine,
And names of the reindeer that wait in line.
But there should be more talk of God's great love,
Which sent baby Jesus, straight from Above

Christmas Is A Birthday (2)
Christ Is In Christmas (2)

(Written in a meter of ..-..-..-..-)
Anapest Tetrameter
12 syllables in 36 rhyming lines

Now, the night before Christmas that is Christmas Eve.
It's a birthday, but not one of Adam and Eve
There's a magic in air, but no card up your sleeve,
For the greatness of magic is when you believe.
    It's Christ's birth, and a gift Mary had to conceive.
    And a promise that sin's guilt He came to relieve.
    At this time Santa knows if a child is naughty,
    Or is nice enough to get some gifts and party.
More than gifts, we have Jesus, faith, family and food.
All of these put together are the Christmas mood.
There are helpers of Santa who do volunteer,
And whose job is to spread some of that Christmas cheer.
    Please don't misunderstand, 'cause cheer doesn't mean beer,
    But it means we remove loss of hope and its fear.
    And we do that by reminding all those who care
    That each Christmas it means you get gifts and you share.
And we know Christ gets lost in the tinsel and lights,
Also, He can be lost in the stress and the fights.
But He's found once again when we find Silent Night,
Which allows Christ in Christmas to our great delight.
    Christmas time means a break from our work or our school,
    And we emphasize then to all The Golden Rule.
    We have shopping, and Christmas trees with ornaments,
    But "Love God" is the first of the Ten Commandments.
Don't you worry about Santa Claus or his sleigh.
You just try to do your best and try to obey.
For what is better than getting a Christmas card?
It's the keeping of Christ in Christmas; that's not hard.

After eating a meal we watch shows on TV,
Or we read some new book, or just talk pleasantly.
Just remember to thank God for all of His gifts.
And the gift that is Christ is the gift that still lifts.
So don't talk of the reindeer, and Rudolph's nose shine,
Or the names of the reindeer all standing in line,
Talk of Jesus, and talk of God's really great love,
Which gave us baby Jesus who came from Above.

Free Verse
Love Rhymes

(Written in a meter of .-.-.-.-)
Iambic Tetrameter
8 syllables in 32 lines of mostly free verse

This is the sound of just free verse,
As it speaks of love and beauty,
And of the difference that sex makes.
Free verse will tell us everything,
    And anything that deals with this,
    From a girl's breasts with sheer beauty
    To the allure of her figure,
    Her silky hair, and her perfume.
And free verse also speaks of: shoes,
Her clothes, makeup and warm presence,
And curvy hips and luscious lips,
His manly frame and big muscles,
    And having the gift of good health,
    Pure virtue, and the joy of youth.
    Free verse without rhyme sounds like this.
    It does involve you and your miss,
And what is said involves us all.
The use of free verse may be fine,
Because there's no rhyme in the line,
Except a few lines that may rhyme.
    But I've used free verse just to show,
    And now I think it's time to go,
    'Cause I've lost what that sound should be.
    These lines all rhyme now, certainly.
If you thought free verse is this one,
This poem with which we've begun
To explore the use of free verse,
I don't think it could end much worse.

'Cause it talks of love and delight,
And stolen kisses in the night,
While sitting close in the moonlight,
For love rhymes, and it rhymes just right.

Love Draws
So Find It

(Written in a meter of .-.-.-.-)
Iambic Tetrameter
8 syllables in 32 rhyming lines

All love attracts like strong magnets,
And what it wants it always gets.
For love draws couples together,
And doesn't mind the bad weather.
    It's sensitive like an artist,
    With beauty no one can resist.
    It may seem new or may seem quaint,
    But love's got faith, just like a Saint.
It's subtle, how it can insist.
And love will stay; it will persist.
Love has the wisdom of the wise,
It can't be ever otherwise.
    And love has great humility;
    A child's adaptability,
    And a flower's fragility,
    Plus, athlete like agility.
Humans are made in love's image.
This keeps our balance on the edge.
Love has more value than money,
And love's much sweeter than honey.
    Look to find love in everyone,
    Without love there could be no fun.
    Love has the joy of certainty.
    It can't act patronizingly.
Like banks, it's made for deposits.
What philosophers know, it fits.
Love understands like a scholar.
Its value's more than our dollar.

Love comes from God, for God is love.
Thank God we have love from Above.
Without love we would all be lost.
So find it, 'cause it's worth the cost.

A Ring
You Are Beloved

(Written in a meter of .-.-)
Iambic Dimeter
4 syllables in 44 rhyming lines

To lose a ring
Is no small thing.
Especially,
Since rings aren't free,
    And some have meant
    Great sentiment.
    A mistake's made.
    Plan to upgrade.
The shock of loss
Gives pain of course.
Anxiety's
A certainty.
    What should be done,
    When you lose one?
    Take out a loan?
    Just fret and moan?
No, you report;
Express your hurt,
Then carry on;
Your feelings sort.
    You have support.
    Keep up your chin.
    You still can win.
    Just hold your fort.
God won't abort.
He loves us all.
You cannot fall.
To Him you call.

Next Mineral show,
Make plans to go.
Please see life's scope.
Don't give up hope.
Just ride the wave.
God still can save.
Stay brave; don't rave.
Each crook's a knave.
       You may feel pain
       Now, and again,
       But this I know,
       You are loved so
That we'll take time
To make this rhyme
That shows you're loved.
And are beloved.

This was written in support of a granddaughter who lost her ring at a movie theater.

Leading Like New Stars
Love Needs An Other

(Written in a meter of ..-..-..-..-)
Anapest Tetrameter
12 syllables in 32 rhyming lines

G. K. Chesterton found that the East and the West
Had some symbols that summarized beliefs the best.
Chinese Buddhists in temples had beliefs they held,
Opposite to beliefs of what Christians upheld.
    Christian Crosses extended to reach out to all
    With a central crossroads contradiction like call.
    The center's stable starting point calls without cease.
    Jesus said He did not come on earth to bring peace.
Jesus came on earth to bring a sword that can cut,
And divide, separate, take a stand, all that, but
That meant creed boundaries, and not doubt, be set down.
This division relates you with those not your own,
    For real love needs a personality to love.
    Separation of souls is design from Above.
    A real love lays its life down, and ends in bloodshed.
    Now, the Buddhists they tolerate all roads instead,
And they end with themselves, finally nothingness.
Christians search for their true home, and for nothing less.
And these Christians have eyes open, as they look out.
Their four direction Cross shows what they're all about.
    Buddhists sit with eyes-closed, for they're inward looking,
    And that's a symbol of what is called contracting.
    Other Buddhist's symbols are a circle that's closed,
    Or a snake swallowing its tail, fixed and enclosed.
Resurrection gives you your own body, that's true.
Reincarnation doesn't give the same to you.
It seems East and the West cannot get together
Except through Jesus, who is to all a brother.

East and West came together once with the Wise Men,
Who brought frankincense, gold and some myrrh with them, then.
These were symbols of Jesus as: God, King and man.
Like new stars, Christians lead to Jesus in God's plan.

Adventure Or Romance
Live To Love

(Written in a meter of .-.-.-.-)
Iambic Tetrameter
8 syllables in 52 rhyming lines

When you give love, you give yourself.
So I should first study myself,
Before moving to something more.
What I am, I just can't ignore.
    We're often given one great chance
    To find adventure or romance.
    Adventure's risky and thrilling,
    Also, stirring and exciting.
Romance has all of the above,
Plus: relation, ardor, and love.
To make a choice is hard we're told.
Should we save or savor the world?
    Love does affect decision time.
    It's influence is very prime
    For it guides us just all the time.
    In fact, it puts it all in rhyme.
Adventure goes to outer space,
Or an exotic foreign place.
Lovers ask each, "What should I do?
Help me decide, for I love you?"
    If you don't live to love, I know,
    You won't love to live; that is so.
    Miss out on love; miss out on life.
    My life's adventure is my wife.
A spouse is understandably
So yearned for irresistibly,
And this desire, when you inquire,
Is irresistible desire.

Love that you keep is love you give,
And that is one great way to live.
For lovers get reward, you see,
By their rewarding constantly.
True love has been called a madness,
But cure is loss with love sickness.
To those afflicted you can tell
That they don't want to be made well.
Love gives us special seeing eyes
To bring alive beauty in skies.
True love floats you to walk a cloud,
For love is peaceful and not loud.
Time not spent on love is wasted,
Even love predestinated.
True lovers find themselves bonded
For they are not simply mated.
Two minus one is found nothing,
But one plus one is everything.
Love of one beats applause from all
That is important to recall.
To any question in your mind,
True love's the answer, all hearts find.
You never lose your way back home
To those you love, after you roam.

Can We Just Talk A While?
I Hear You're Seeking Me

(Written in a meter of .-.-.-)
Iambic Trimeter
6 syllables in 40 alternate rhyming lines

"We have met already,
In my dreams every night.
I hear you're seeking me.
My name is Mr. Right.
    You seem so unaware,
    You're living poetry.
    You're answer to my prayer.
    Your devotee, that's me.
You look to me right now,
Just like my future wife.
I'm trying to somehow,
Include you in my life.
    I've been asked to escort
    You from out of this room.
    For other girls report
    They look bad; out of bloom."
"Listen big boy to me.
We've not been introduced.
Your name is mystery.
To leave, I'm not induced.
    And Mr. Right, I know,
    Would not use any line.
    He tends to work real slow
    With truthful words just fine.
So please heed what I say.
Just simply go away!
For chips fall where they may,
And yours have gone astray."

"My name is James Armstrong.
Please let me start anew.
Forgive me, I've been wrong.
Please help me to know you.
We go to the same school.
You pass me in the hall.
Can we just talk a while?
On you I'd like to call."
    "I said to go away.
Now, I think you should stay.
We both feel the same way.
Fate brought us close today."

There's A Way To Know
All This Is Proof

(Written in Free Verse)
8 syllables in each of 32 lines

How do I know that I love you?
'Cause my love makes me know much more,
Than I have ever known before.
I'm jealous and that shows my love.
    Little by little love's presence
    Helped me find something like essence.
    I found what I did want to find,
    Although I knew not what to seek
Now I don't taste, but savor life.
I don't just see, but I observe.
And I feel wise; fully alive.
I don't just know, but understand.
    There is no love unless there's trust.
    I've love, which is the greatest force.
    You are my friend in whom I trust.
    We both are looking the same way.
The beauty of it is just this:
My love it wills to share your pain,
And find for you your greatest good.
I want us not to be apart.
    I've found that love's the loudest sound
    On the other side of silence.
    Our silent touch means more than words.
    I feel that you've captured my heart.
I now have moments that mean all,
Instead of years that mean nothing.
And one and one means everything.
Each kiss is a timeless moment.

Applause from you means more to me
Than all the applause from the world.
All this is proof that I love you.
Now, how do you know you love me?

Shoved By A Kiss
Sexual Desire Fire

(Written in a meter of .-.-.- and .-.-)
Iambic trimeter and Iambic bimeter
18 lines of 6 syllables alternating with 4 syllables that rhyme

A sexual desire
 Can burn like fire
Of sexual delight
 That feels just right.
And this delightful urge
 May have a surge,
And for a kiss insist,
 Which will persist.
It's so hard to resist,
 And can't be missed.
A kiss may start it all,
 I mean your fall.
For you can fall in love
 From its strong shove.
The other way around
 Is often found,
You fall in love at first,
 Then, have kiss thirst.

Life

Beloved

People Poke And Pratfall
Laughter

(Written in a meter of .-.-.-.-)
Iambic Tetrameter
8 syllables in 20 lines

From mistaken identity
To satire and parody,
Or double-talk, or runaround,
There's humor there that can be found
    The timing of just when to pause
    Can be quite funny, just because,
    We all can be in on the joke
    With humor that can people poke
Outlandish situations still
Make us laugh loud against our will.
Slapstick is classic, with pratfall,
To bring out laughter from us all.
    To just make up a funny face,
    Or act like you are out of place,
    Seems to bring out some joy in us.
    Our laughter adds to life a plus.
All humor we need to embrace.
Throughout our lives we find a trace.
Try to add to it all you can
And soon you'll be its biggest fan.

Pushing The Envelope
But It's Stationery

(Written in a meter of .-.-.-.-)
Iambic Tetrameter
8 syllables in 20 rhyming lines

I'll promulgate, relate and state,
And narrate and enunciate,
"I tried to push the envelope.
It's stationery, so I mope."
    I know it will take more than hope
    I can't succeed with just a rope,
    'Cause I can't even push my luck.
    Do you think that I've been dumbstruck?
I can not even find for us
another word for Thesaurus.
The long word, "abbreviated,"
Means that a short word is stated.
    Apartments, they are together.
    They're not apart, as I infer.
    "Why does my skin get dark in sun,
    And hair get light," that's my question?
There's a lot I don't understand,
Unless you take me by my hand,
With better pictures to portray
To guide me how to see today,

Experience
Beauty Is Not Known By Proxy

28 lines of Free Verse

What composition is for an artist
Experience is for the body.
Both are something that's very basic.
Consider the basic experience of a sunset.
>   Poets can't fully put that into words,
>   Even after they've had that experience.
>   And artists can't paint the full glory of it,
>   Because everything except experience
Is just a kind of reflection
That's seen in a cloudy mirror,
As a kind of stand-in or a sort of proxy
That's standing-in for sublime awe, wonder and glory.
>   Experience is so much more than hearsay or
>   description..
>   It is enjoying the gourmet meal
>   Instead of just reading the menu.
>   And taking the journey instead of reading the
>   tour book.
Experience is not confusing symbol with reality,
Nor confusing money with true wealth.
And not letting the time on a watch tell you
When your body is hungry.
>   For beauty to be fully and completely
>   known,
>   The experience of beauty must be
>   experienced.
>   Experience is like vivid colors of paint,
>   Compared to just a black and white drawing,
Even if the hand of a Raphael moved the pencil.
Until there is first an experience,
Then there is nothing to reflect or show,
And nothing there to fully know.

It's Been Said
Memorable

52 lines of free verse

Frankly my dear.....
Tomorrow is another day.
I heard it on the grapevine.
That does not compute.
    Do you want fries with that?
    Shaken but not stirred.
    Where's the beef?
    Stay thirsty my friend.
There's not going to be a rematch.
I don't want one.
The Italian Stallion
Yo Adrian! Rocky!
    Forget about it.
    Come and get it wiseguy.
    It's the cops.
    I'll be back!
I'm singing in the rain.
Or else the terrorists win.
Come and meet my little friend!
Go ahead and make my day!
    I know what you're thinking.
    Do you feel lucky, punk?
    We'll make him an offer he can't refuse.
    Play it again Sam.
Why ask for the moon, when we have the stars?
It's time for a showdown.
Load up men and let's ride.
Go ahead and draw.
    Don't move! I've got you covered.
    Drop that gun!
    Who's on first?
    Life finds a way.

Come and get me copper!
Aim for the whites of their eyes.
May the force be with you.
You don't know who you're dealing with, that's Rambo.
    Let's eat!
    Don't go around hungry.
    Nuts!
    Wax on, wax off
A penny for your thoughts.
Look up in the sky! It's a bird. It's a plane.
Elementary my dear Watson.
Hi ho Silver, away!
    It's real quiet, too quiet.
    Freeze!
    I've got a plan.
    Here they come!
Don't bring a knife to a gunfight.
We're not in Kansas anymore, Toto.
Follow the yellow brick road
The family that prays together, stays together

Surviving Inflation
The Rich Man Turned Away

(Written in a meter of .-.-.-.-)
Iambic Tetrameter
8 syllables in 40 rhyming lines

Inflation prices, when they're high,
So high they reach up to the sky,
We're told then, "Buy, no need to sulk,
On sale, in season, and in bulk."
    We're also told, so we won't lack,
    "Conserve, reduce and just cut back
    Drive less so gas prices may fall."
    It hasn't worked that way at all.
Despite what we've tried and been told,
Eroding income hurts the old.
And "Penny" candy costs much more,
Than it has ever cost before,
    We're all in need of a big raise,
    Or lower taxes that each pays.
    I now see that the thing to fear
    Is running out of cash; that's near.
How come folks still buy cigarettes,
And even place down all their bets?
They can afford to buy their beer.
These facts of life they're not so clear.
    I think that soon the luxury
    I can't afford will be TV.
    I've cancelled out my newspaper.
    I have the sense I don't prosper.
Is someone there who is to blame,
Some politician you can name?
"Are living standards much too high,
Or are the world's too low?," we cry.

High living standards can abuse.
Reduce, recycle and reuse.
Use energy renewable.
Keep everything sustainable.
Don't call it "living" with two jobs
To make money to live like snobs.
With moms who don't stay home with kids,
Which puts their future up for bids.
The Bible talks of stewardship,
And God's love and His partnership.
And how the rich man turned away,
Despite what God told him that day.

Retirement Or Re-tirement
Rest Or Re-creation

(Written in a meter of ..-..-..-..-)
Anapest Tetrameter
12 syllables in 28 rhyming lines

Twenty years of hard work should give you retirement.
At some jobs, now, retirement is not what is meant.
You're let go before that, and for any good cause.
All because your retirement cost gives bosses pause.
    The rest and recreation of our "Golden Years"
    Won't occur how we thought; and that now is our fears.
    Post-retirement career's not an oxymoron,
    It's "next step" in "third age" some folks are banking on.
We tend to think of two choices, work or get fired.
There is, also, work 'til you drop or you're retired.
Now, retirement does not have to mean that you're tired.
It can mean that you now work at home being "wired."
    To retire can mean change of job for renewal,
    Trying new things, like travel and some accrual.
    We are part of Longevity Revolution,
    Which means our life expectancy has addition.
We're now free from our work, and are now free to work
At what we've always wanted to do at this fork.
Each of our lives can be a big contribution,
Instead of an entitlement situation.
    We can make an alternate story folks will tell
    Of encore-career octo-hotties doing well.
    We've got civil rights, women's rights, now there's gray rights.
    These are rights to solve problems, and join "geezer" fights.
Elder generation can be agent of change.
They have knowledge and wisdom that covers great range.
Having their gift of time, they'll need to be engaged.
How this time will be spent is where change will be waged.

Haunted House In The Woods
A Campfire Tale

(Written in a meter of .-.-.-.-)
Iambic Tetrameter
8 syllables alternating with 6 in a Ballad style of 72 lines
The 6-syllable lines rhyme

When you go on a camping trip
    Into the deep forest,
At night around the old campfire,
    This scary story's best.

There is a nearby haunted house,
    Deserted, dark and old.
You're dared to go and walk right in,
    To show you're brave and bold,

You go to an upstairs window
    To wave to those outside.
And then alone, come out again,
    To hear cheers at your side.

The first time you do it of course,
    You are the last to go.
Five friends of yours each take their turn.
    They all look full of woe.

At the upstairs front windowsill,
    They wave to you below.
This all is done about midnight.
    Their waves will all seem slow.

A flashlight is their only light,
    Please try to hold yours tight.
Scared faces that reflect real bright,
    You'll recall from that night.

It went, exactly, just as planned,
    Except for one great flaw.
My five friends they each got their turn,
    And each of them I saw.

But then their flashlights each went out;
    Each followed by a scream.
It happened to all five of them,
    And seemed like a bad dream.

Of all the five that did go in
    Not one came out again.
To only enter and not leave
    Was quite a bad bargain.

It now was my turn to go in.
    My prospects seemed quite slim.
For me to go in search of them
    Could make me a victim.

I didn't want to take my turn.
    Great fear in me did burn.
Yet, I could not stand there alone,
    And stay scared to the bone.

I slowly pushed on the front door
    It creaked and opened wide.
My searchlight searched to find the stairs
    For I was now inside.

It was real dark and quite eerie,
    And then I heard a sound.
It was the creaking of the stairs,
    As upstairs I did bound.

I entered the upstairs bedroom,
    Which has the front window.
The moonlight that was coming in
    Created a shadow.

I turned to see what could make it,
    Then came a great loud noise.
It was the sound of: "Hey! Surprise!,"
    Which came from all the boys.

They all had pulled a trick on me,
    Pretending they were killed.
They waited in the dark, and then,
    When I came in they yelled.

When you tell this at a campfire
    Try to arrange a noise.
For when folks listen real intense,
    A noise will shake their poise.

What works is if you just shout out.
    What's next no one can tell.
To make this clear I'll say flat-out,
    "Just simply start to yell!"

Two Categories
Being Labeled

(Written in a meter of .-.-.-.-)
Iambic Tetrameter
8 syllables in 32 rhyming lines

During my youth the movies had
A label "B" for shows thought "bad."
No movie stars led those stories,
For stars led "A" categories.
    Lesser known actors played "B" leads,
    But they did all the same brave deeds,
    As all of the same swashbucklers,
    Who were in the "A" blockbusters.
Blockbuster got that name, because
The ticket-line length found there was
Over a block long due to fame
Of the stars who drew those who came.
    A big audience was the game.
    So movie star's fame with big name
    Was cultivated, advertised,
    And honored, and was greatly prized.
Now, this star system all is gone.
That fact you should not dwell upon,
'Cause publicity brings the same.
Plus, other things that I will name.
    They are named notoriety,
    And scandal, and some nudity;
    Adultery and some divorce,
    And many other things, of course.
Included in advertising
Are these and what their shock can bring.
Actors try to get out this word,
If their fame has not yet occurred.

We still do name things "A" and "B,"
What "B" means has changed, certainly,
"B" is now "evil;" "A" is "good."
What both are is quite understood.

Picture A Time
A Missing Link

(Written in a meter of .-.-.-.-)
Iambic Tetrameter
8 syllables in 24 rhyming lines

Picture a time of problems solved.
A future time of life evolved,
Where everyone has perfect looks,
And access to all that's in books.
    Disease has been conquered at last,
    And distance is traveled real fast.
    It's now called super fast, and more,
    And love's honored in each one's core.
Whatever's good takes an encore.
There's peace at last, and there's no war.
And food's available for all.
And no one ever can just fall.
    What I know of the human race,
    There never can be such a place,
    For evil stops it being so.
    There's good and evil, this we know.
But if evil can be removed,
Then life on earth would be improved.
We'd call it "heaven," don't you think?
That's why we hope we're near that brink.
    But we still have a missing link.
    Please, find it or our hopes will sink.
    To fight all evil we must learn,
    That to our God we first must turn.

On The Brink
What I Think

(Written in a meter of .-.-.-.-)
Iambic Tetrameter
8 syllables in 20 rhyming lines

Do you want to know what I think?
I think the world is on the brink,
In such a way that it might sink,
Unless we find our missing link.
    What's missing comes as no surprise,
    There seems no way to compromise.
    Progressive liberals, they fight
    Conservatives, there on the right.
There's back and forth we all can note,
Whenever it comes time to vote.
It's not just us, nations fight too.
I don't know what we all can do,
    Except perhaps turn back to God,
    And start to pray and not just nod.
    So go ahead, let's hear you pray,
    And not tomorrow, now, today!
For that sweet sound will calm my fears,
As we all pray throughout the years.
There's something we need understand,
With God is where we all must stand.

Resolve To Revolve
Feel The Wheel

(Written in a meter of .-.-.-.-)
Iambic Tetrameter
8 syllables in 40 rhyming lines

To go through a revolving door
May be something you've done before,
But this is the first time for me.
I stand in line here patiently.
    I think it could cause vertigo.
    But I still think I'd like to go,
    And push a door that makes a swish.
    It's something that's become my wish.
One axis holds four doors in place.
The speed of turning has a pace
That's set by surging crowds today,
Who rush to push each door away.
    Doors pirouette and they rotate.
    They turn and spin, and they gyrate,
    In cycles that recur, you know,
    To let people go in with flow.
Of Russian Roulette I do think,
As my turn comes close to the brink.
For a revolving cylinder
Is what could make my death occur.
    I'm now caught in the door's orbit.
    There is no place to stop or sit.
    Rotation has become my fate.
    My speed of walking isn't late.
I push and whirl myself around,
And hope I don't fall to the ground.
I feel the wheel of fate abound.
I'm circumnavigation bound.

I stay in place within the twist.
The roll I'm in seems to insist.
I circumduct and end up where
I'm outside, again, in the air.
I know now for my survival
The periodic interval,
For when I must step out of there,
Which is what you must be aware.
I make it through to get inside.
My friends they all are at my side.
"Let's go again, and then later,
We'll find a fast escalator."

* (This was written in tribute and in memory of a
granddaughter's first revolving door experience)

Three Watches
It's All Downhill

(Written in a meter of .-.-.-.-)
Iambic tetrameter
8 syllables in 16 rhyming lines

Three men climbed up a slanted hill,
And at the top stood very still.
A certain challenge had been made,
And that's why they went up that grade.
    The challenge had to do with time.
    You'll find what that was in this rhyme.
    The first threw his watch far away.
    Now it can't work, it broke that day.
The next man, call him, "number two."
He threw his watch, and it broke too.
The third man threw his watch, and walked
Straight down the hill, while others talked.
    He then caught his watch in the air.
    The first two said, "That is not fair.
    How could you catch your watch below?"
    "I can because my watch runs slow."

School Supplies
Home With A Fever

(Written in a meter of .-.-.-.-)
Iambic Tetrameter
8 syllables in 28 rhyming lines

Three children are in my family
Jessica, Jonathan and me.
There are no school supplies we need.
Right now that's true; it is indeed.
    We go to school and try to learn,
    If getting sick is not our turn.
    My cousin Sarah takes the bus,
    But sometime she comes home with us.
By "us" I mean grandpa and me.
He drives us when my mom's not free.
The trip from school to home's not far.
School bus takes longer than the car.
    I'm going home now grandpa's way.
    He picked me up at school today.
    That allowed mom at home to stay.
    My sick brother in bed must lay.
But his fever is coming down.
He's now all smiles without a frown.
We all catch germs from whatever.
These germs can give us a fever.
    Sometimes a fever's serious,
    Enough that you're delirious.
    I'm Christina who's talking here.
    I'm a good girl without a fear.
When I get home I grab a snack,
Then take homework from my backpack.
I thank grandpa for what he does.
He's the greatest that ever was.

Oil, Dollars, and Real Value
Stagflation

(Written in meter of .-.-.-.-)
Iambic Tetrameter
8 syllables in 52 rhyming lines

We're in a hole, let's stop digging.
By digging I mean our spending.
Our debt owes interest money;
That's wasted money, don't you see?
    To print money it devalues
    Dollars, so stop printing or lose.
    When oil prices go up, it's known,
    That's when dollar value goes down.
The graphs show this fact very nice.
All prices rise to match oil's price.
We all have mostly what we need.
High prices make for money bleed.
    That cost can bring a country down,
    Especially when debt's around.
    So, energy independence
    Our country needs to evidence.
Stagflation is stagnant wages
With rising prices and taxes.
This leads to what's called recession.
That's become the latest fashion.
    We can't afford to buy things then,
    That causes jobless deflation.
    Give us a raise; lower taxes.
    Only freeze prices not wages.
More waste is violence and war.
Find those not paying their fair share.
Some greedy schemers bleed systems.
Eliminate tax exemptions.

Our complex tax code's outdated.
Let's find out where money's wasted.
The world contains greed and evil,
But there are hungry mouths to fill.
Let's use our money wisely, then,
For schools, teachers, and firemen,
Police and the military,
And for what makes public safety.
Another use for our monies
Is for political parties.
They need to do a better job,
And stop their acting like a mob.
So let us balance the budget.
We're near default, don't you forget.
Our life can seem hard when we can't
Get everything at once we want.
If we can't agree, how can we
Get other countries to agree?
All things have cost, 'cause they're not free.
What comes first is stable money.
Love can bring a radical shift
From love of money to sane thrift.
Let's start to live within our means,
And put God's values in these scenes.

A Good Guy's Hat
Good Example To See

(Written in a meter of .-.-.-.-)
Iambic Tetrameter
8 syllables in 20 rhyming lines

You may not find any new cure,
Drug or device, now that's for sure.
You'll always be much more than that,
Because you wear your "good guys" hat.
 Believe me that is hard to do,
 And it looks very good on you.
 You may never win a big prize,
 But you've seen love in someone's eyes.
You've helped your family hold true,
And helped folks who were feeling blue.
A life like that is just pure gold;
A most lovely sight to behold.
 Don't ever put that hat away.
 We all should wear ours every day.
 Please know that you inspire me.
 Good example is what I see.
In life's journey you're a treasure,
Who makes me rich beyond measure.
You're not aware how much you teach,
By your example, which does preach.

Beautiful Human Flowers
All They Can Be

(Written in a meter of ..-..-..-..-)
Anapest Tetrameter
12 syllables in 16 lines with alternate lines rhyming

There are beautiful people who are like flowers,
With a beauty inside, and a beauty outside.
And these flowers can be only just what they are,
With a beauty that's there, seen or not, without pride.
    Their sweet fragrance is left where they blossom and bloom.
    And it does not depend on someone being there,
    Because when there is no one to see, God still does.
    And His recognition needs no one be aware.
This great beauty needs not to compare or depend
On the beauty of other flowers in the field.
For their beautiful spirit depends not at all
On what others may think or a circumstance yield.
    They're not thought of as rare, but unique as witness.
    They remind us of God's likeness, most certainly.
    Each stands out independently, and all alone.
    They are happy with just being all they can be.

We All Need Mercy
Wrath's Not A Path

(Written in a meter of .-.-.-.-)
Iambic Tetrameter
8 syllable in 36 alternately rhyming lines

A good son once gave a loud shout,
Against a brother he thought won.
The angry older son cried out,
Against who's called, "Prodigal Son."
    But old sons are prodigal, too.
    Relationship is what they lose,
    For God has made it all for you,
    And anger hurts how you will choose.
Now Jonah thought some folks deserved
To not go free, and was annoyed
That what had been for them reserved
Did not happen; they weren't destroyed.
    The folks of Nineveh it seems,
    Our Jonah disliked, so he flees.
    He won't help do one of God's schemes;
    Get Nineveh upon its knees.
God's people have it in their means
By talk to have others repent,
If sent by God right to the scenes
To do His will at where they're sent.
    Relent and do just what God asks,
    Or risk three days within a fish.
    Some need that to perform their tasks.
    Accomplish, now, and don't just wish.
The lessons to be found in this:
Be grateful that you do not get
What anger deserves. It's not bliss.
God gets what He wants, don't forget.

And God gets it with help from us,
But we need to listen to Him.
God stomachs a lot of our fuss.
Do what He asks, not just your whim.
Our enemies may deserve wrath,
But what we all need is mercy.
Don't let wrath be your chosen path.
Self-righteous revenge must not be.

Eat Right Or You'll Be Left
Passing On

(Written in a meter of .-.-.-.-)
Iambic Tetrameter
8 syllables in 20 rhyming lines

To eat right we must be conformed,
But some of us are uninformed.
Those are the ones who'll get infirm.
That's something we can all confirm.
    We all would be quite dead of course,
    Without a doctor and a nurse.
    That's why I want to thank them all.
    They're always at our beck and call.
You may have high cholesterol;
Ingest high fats, plus alcohol,
With sugar, and with lots of salt,
And then claim that it's not your fault.
    But we folks who are in the know,
    Suggest a better way to go.
    We learned it from research that's done,
    And passed on to us one to one.
You should not smoke at all of course,
It only tends to make things worse.
For some, great changes must be made
Before I can end this tirade.

Humor
Joie de Vivre

(Written in a meter of .-.-.-.-)
Iambic Tetrameter
8 syllables in 28 rhyming lines

Some humor flows from ironies,
And contradictions, parodies.
How things are, were, or ought to be
Gives humor its variety.
    Some disagreement's useful too.
    There's wisdom there that's meant for you.
    Use humor to just people poke.
    Don't make fun of them, that's no joke.
Find crusty or misunderstood.
Exaggerate is also good
To make us laugh or give a smile.
All jokes aside, it's all worthwhile.
    Incongruousness and foibles
    Gets laughs, because they turn tables.
    Hyperbole, when used as wit,
    Can give us all some jokes that fit.
All levity gives enjoyment,
Which gives to life some enhancement.
Release endorphins; open jaw,
Find for yourself *joie de vivre*.
    When humor's used as a defense,
    Its benefits are quite immense.
    There's laughs in putting on pretense,
    And also humor in suspense.
In fact, some humor's everywhere.
And it will help you if you care
To use its joy to lift your life,
And elevate it above strife.

Rock
Where To Build

(Written in a meter of .-.-.-)
Iambic Trimeter
6 syllables in 36 alternately rhyming lines

With every act you do,
You're building up your life.
Please listen to this clue
To help avoid some strife.
    Please build upon a rock.
    Don't ever build on sand.
    Of Jesus, please take stock.
    He's Rock on where to stand.
For the Bible calls Him
Our Rock of Salvation.
Without Him life is dim.
Make Him your rock station.
    Without Him, when a storm
    Arrives, you'll sink in sand.
    Sand tries hard to conform.
    Please, try to understand.
Sand can be what you whim
That can take you away
From being close to Him.
So please heed what I say.
    Since sand is anything,
    It could be your career,
    Or "love of money" thing.
    Its loss is what you fear.
A life like that can't rhyme.
Plus, don't seek for revenge.
It's such a waste of time,
When you try to avenge.

So seek love as your Rock,
And seek forgiveness, too.
The words I speak don't knock.
It's truth that's meant for you.
Relate all these to Him:
Time, talent and treasure.
Life's joy, don't make it grim.
God gives in full measure.

A Sinner
Trying to Bless

(Written in a meter of .-.-.-.-)
Iambic Tetrameter
8 syllables in 16 rhyming lines

I fail, and fail, and fail, and fail.
And then what do I do, just wail.
Our lives must surely more entail
Than life in jail lived without bail.
    If God were not here I'd be lost,
    For He has shown to me the cost
    Of having faith and finding love,
    And knowing truth we've all heard of.
It's true, unless I miss my guess,
Our God wants faithful, not success.
And so my sins I do confess.
Then I try to make my life bless.
    A trinity I fully see
    That may have once eluded me.
    We've spirit with body and mind,
    To guides us, and our God to find.

Body	*Mind*	*Spirit*
Heart	Brain	Soul
Feel	Think	Teach
Sensitive	Intelligent	Wise
Do/Industrious	Say/Speak	Preach/Pray
Beautiful	True	Inspired/Good
Artist/Poet	Philosopher	Prophet/Priest
Emotional	Logical	Moral/Spiritual

Woman	*Man*	*Nature*
Sensual	Rational	Organic
Emotional	Reasonable	Inorganic
Subjective	Objective	Neutral
East	West	Global

Consolation	*Desolation*	*Transformation*
Joy	Sorrow	Wisdom/Virtue
Comfort	Suffering	Meaning/Purpose
Pleasure	Pain	Happiness
City	Desert	Garden

The Story Of A Well
A Close Encounter

(Written in a meter of .-.-.-.-)
Iambic Pentameter
10 syllables in 28 rhyming lines

The Bible tells the story of a well,
And of a girl nearby it, who did dwell.
She goes to get some water for her thirst,
And Jesus is there, 'cause He gets there first.
    He has a thirst for souls that is His own,
    And His request for drink she can't turn down.
    Both Jesus and the well have depth indeed,
    And that's exactly what this girl does need.
She sees her life through her dear Savior's eyes,
And leaves her jug, and to her town she flies.
She tells them that Messiah now is here,
And that gets rid of anything they fear.
    The world had thirst for this event to come.
    And many lives reformed was the outcome.
    Now many will encounter Him today,
    And get refreshed by what He has to say.
In truth and spirit He is found always.
You can encounter Him on busy days.
Your thirst will find that He's living water.
Don't thirst again, have your own encounter.
    God wills that you'll find His love and mercy.
    His broken heart it flowed on Calvary
    With blood and water like a great fountain.
    This love and mercy floods us all since then
When Jesus was born there were three wise men,
And also shepherds, who were nearby then.
These wise and simple ones found Him, each knows,
But He can find us, as this story shows.

Greed
Being Blunt

(Written in a meter of .-.-.-.-)
Iambic Tetrameter
6 syllables in 12 alternately rhyming lines

God gives us everything.
His price is just effort.
We freely laugh and sing,
Cry, suffer and comfort.
    Is there more that we need,
    Or is our lack just want?
    We're all greedy indeed.
    That fact is true and blunt.
Our greed we should confess.
God loves you, please recall.
Find truth, love and goodness,
With that, you'll have it all.

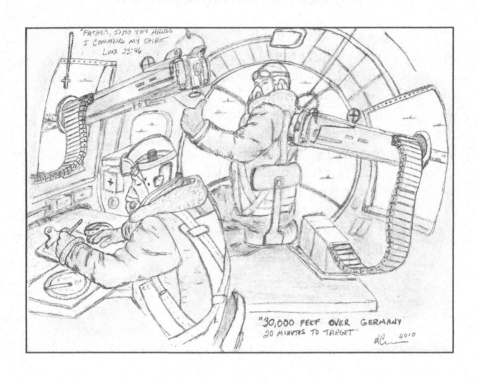

30,000 Feet Over Germany
20 minutes to target
Father into Thy hands I commend my spirit
-Luke 23:46
(Art by artist Kit Cessna 2010)

Poems By
My Family

Carnival Lights
Daydreams
Claire Holahan   Age 19

(Written in a meter of -..-..-..-)
dactyl tetrameter
10 syllables in 16 rhyming lines

Carnival lights are too bright for my eyes
Blocking out stars decorating night skies
Gardens are blooming without any care
Call out, my sweet, and you know I'll be there

Singing about girls in satin white gowns
Laundromat change and bright cavalcade clowns
Burning the city wherever they go
Slowly they waltz where the red angels grow

Masquerade litters the streets in these days.
A man parades the skies with hopeful gaze,
Blinking a few times, recalling a dream
City of hope, where all are as they seem

Then I close your eyes with whispers of bed
Tomorrow brings dust and skin that's been shed
If you could live without stories I tell
Then child, I would have no daydreams to sell

Dream

Rachel Cessna   age 13

(Written in free verse)
metaphor rich
8 and 6 syllables alternate in 24 lines

I slipped into the deepest sleep,
And then my eyes did dream.
Of song, and time, and life itself,
And thunder, rain, and snow.
　　The magic in the air danced past.
　　The Moon mourned her mother,
　　Who Death did claim last week; too fast
　　Her time on earth did go.
One day alive then passed away.
That's how it is for all.
And Father Time stood up and stretched
"The dawn's coming!" he shouts.
　　To go see every bit of it
　　I stretched my wings and soared.
　　I fly lost over dusty toys,
　　As the day marched onward.
The wind whined for me to hurry.
I'd love to stay longer,
But time, just like a bird, flies past.
And shadow comes take me
　　Back to the world, where I do live.
　　I'll come back here again
　　To visit all of them, my friends.
　　In my safe dreams we'll meet.

How Can I Describe
Rachel Cessna   age 13

(Written in Free Verse)
35 lines

How can I describe the
State of mind
Entered by the singer
By the one whose voice
Echoes
Echoes
Echoes
Echoes
Across the stage
And into your ear
To be
Savored and enjoyed?
How can I describe the
Painter's place in her head
When she makes
A rainbow with the swoops of her brush
Swoops
Swoops
Swoops
Swoops
Over canvas and hearts
Speaking to each person
In a different way?
How can I describe the
Way a Poet's mind twists
Twists
Twists
Twists
Twists
Until a poem is made
Delighting some

Shocking others
And confusing many?
Simple,
I just did!

Spring Sing
Rachel Cessna   age 13

(Written in Free Verse)
Metaphor rich
17 lines

Friend, from winter spring has been reborn.
The birds race the wind, wind whooshes past.
The ground's spongy; wet from fresh rain.
Squish, squish, squish, your feet play.
The land is a trampoline, soft and springy;
The most perfect forest floor.
New life smell creeps up your nose.
You lean back and breathe in.
It rains often, friend, rains cats and dogs,
But spring is like a handful of sand.
The more you hold on, the faster it slips out.
Slips, through slim slits between your fingers.
Slides away,
away away.
Soon spring will be gone,
A whisper in the wind.
And summer will come.

Pond Haiku

Rachel Cessna   age 13

(5-7-5 syllable Haiku)
3 lines

It once was peaceful
All of nature, rock and stone
Then the frogs arrived

Snowflakes
Christina Barta   age 13

(Written in a five-line stanza of a cinquain)
5 lines

Snowflakes

Delicate, White

Swirling, Twirling, Whirling

Dancing through the frozen air

Snowfall

Winter's Confetti
Christina Barta   age 13

(Written in a meter of -..-..-..-)
dactyl tetrameter
metaphor rich
10 syllables in 10 rhyming lines

Snow is a delicate, magical thing
Falling in season, just right before spring.

Snow tumbles earthward, as if in a dance.
It's meant to awe and delight and entrance.

Snow is a fluttering, delicate bird
Landing so softly that nothing is heard.

Snow is an artist, who paints with just white,
Covering landscapes in one single night

Snow is a blanket that covers the earth,
Of course, I'm warmer curled up by my hearth.

Snow Day
Jessica Barta   age 10

16 lines

Thick white gently falling flakes.
Jump out of bed, a new world awaits.
Kids shout for joy.
Everywhere you see snowball throwing boys.
Snowballs fly through the air,
Each one missing me by a hair.
Ow! What? My poor frozen toes!
Same issue with my frosty nose.
Snowmen smile, hand in hand.
The streets are covered in nothing but salt and sand.
Oh, how I love the snow!
The children wish it would never go.
For the adults it's a different issue.
Pass the tissue!
We're going to need another box.
Are there any more pairs of socks?

My Poem

Jonathan Barta   age 6

5 lines

We will, we will rock you,

Tock you

Throw you out of the window.

Play your Nintendo

Do a little bando!

The end.

Bon Voyage
Your Ship Has Come In
Joseph Yadusky

(Written in free verse)
16 lines

Hey buddy, can you spare a care?
Spare change? Sparse change.
News from a head cheerleader; blond coif equals gravitas.
Let's go offense. No offense. No offense taken.
America. Home of the brave.
Afghanistan. Home of the grave.
Whining about tax increases from behind breast implants.
Why should you have a fit,
If I give your dog a biscuit?
Keep your hands where I can see 'em.
Keep your shoes where I can see 'em.
Do you want fries with that? No problem.
Do you want lies with that. No problem.
That's not my problem.
My problem has been Biggie sized.
Even without binoculars you can see the iceberg.

Some Days
Sarah Yadusky   age 13

(Written in Free Verse)
14 lines

Some days we step back,
And look at where we've been.
Some days we look forward
To a time and place we might want to see.
Some days we freeze in place;
We don't want to leave the present moment.
Some days we look towards others,
Thinking their "perfection" will take over our "failure,"
But "we" is talking about the general person."
Because some days, I'm a dreamer, and some days I'm not perfect,
But other days, my life is where it is, and where it's supposed to be,
And as long as I'm happy, so is my life.
So the need for flawlessness or deficiency is ended for me today,
Because some days, just some days, my imperfection actually
    makes me perfect.

Remember
Sarah Yadusky   age 13

(Written in Free Verse)
27 lines

Remember today,
Today right now,
As a day of peace for those we love,
Who risk their lives for all,
And even they may fall.
Remember memories
That we've shared and kept,
Throughout our lives,
With peace and rest.
Remember moments,
The ones you can't even share.
The ones that prove your love,
And prove how much you care;
Sometimes resembling a dove.
Remember him,
Or remember her,
For even though they may be gone,
There will be memories that occur
That cause you to remember them again.
So make sure you don't forget,
Because forgetting is just losing
What you don't want to hear.
So remember today,
Today right now,
As a day of peace for those we love,
Who risk their lives for all,
And even they may fall.

Beautiful Water
Sarah Yadusky   age 13

8 lines

I see the fountain, so fresh and clean.

The water that runs, flows lightly with gleam.

I sit and watch it everyday.

The sun makes it sparkle in so many ways.

It is peaceful and calm, and the sounds are so strong.

It dribbles down the sides so sweetly.

I watch it flow as it goes so neatly.

I love this fountain that I watch so deeply.

Friends Make The World Go Round

Sarah Yadusky   age 13

(Written in a meter of .-.-.-)
Iambic Trimeter
26 lines

Friends make the world go round,
and make a lifetime great.
My friends cause ups not downs,
but sometimes friendships break.
Friends help light shine in me,
and help this world be glee.

Friends make the world go round,
and make a lifetime great.
My friends can act like clowns,
but they are like close mate.
My friends they all trust me,
they all have my respect.
If I were to worry,
they all would have my back.

Friends make the world go round,
and make a lifetime great.
They're close to me like ground.
They keep me from all hate.
They're kind, clever, and sweet,
And help my talents shine.
Friends are there forever,
and cause me to feel free.

So, thanks to you my friends,
I enjoy time with you.
Life's better in the end,
that's what it means, "a friend."

Franklin Haiku
William Yadusky Sr.

(Created by a poet residing in snowy Franklin, Wisconsin)

Snowballs thrown.
Skating upon the ice.
Boots covered.
Up to my neck.

Poster Child
William Yadusky Jr.

(Written in Free Verse)
30 lines

(William says: Poster Child is about the depersonalizing of human beings through statistics or images. We are "programmed" to respond emotionally or economically to a news-reel or sales percentage instead of living with in-person humanity/compassion/love/excellence. We know it's not how we're made to live. The first two lines of the poem, relating to combustion and ignition, is about being stirred to genuine compassion or anger or joy, etc. by some form of media account, instead of the actual instance. For example, being deeply moved by some TV special about September 11th without ever meeting anyone who was involved or impacted. It's like living life through second-hand reports. We don't think that's how life is intended to be lived. When we go to movies, we may laugh, cry, despise, reject, embrace, reconsider, etc, even though we know it's not real. William believes many of us have detached ourselves from others, and placed layers of media in between, to turn reality into entertainment, or turn entertainment into our reality, depending on our emotional needs. We experience joy in "reuniting" with old friends on facebook, and we quip on their birthdays and photos, but we never hear their voices or, often, see their actual faces again.)

Perfectly sublime combustion,
echoes of previous ignition;
that I could even stomach the differential
is judgment against this sphere.

Origins of metaphor,
and sources of experience;
many and tens of many,
none real.

Along this diameter of sustenance
where I and they are;
we together are unaware
and inconsiderate of each other.
You are to me simply an implication;

a presumption,
a statistic that is cement;
an observation not requiring a soul.

I...I,

See your eyes.
and

See myself.
and

Feel warmth.
and

Feel touch.
and

Apologize.

For me.
And everyone.
And me more.

Visage
William Yadusky Jr.

(Written in Free Verse)
28 lines

(William says: Visage is about how living, gifted human beings have a
lifetime of opportunity to express goodness, but also, we need to experience
the good as well. And it's about an abstracted telling of an experience that
William had which was very refreshing/inspiring. He was looking at a
stand of huge hardwood trees covered in thin ice, backlit with moonlight
that was behind thin ice clouds, so it was like viewing a really dim x-ray
with accents of diamond brilliance.)

When the ice shell
encrusts the atmosphere of the womb,
and the subordinate orb
sepia, and brushed, appears,
though but a reflection of other glory,
to the terrestrial creatures,
reaching upward,
gnarled, naked, blind, and frozen,
and the marvel is revealed
to other creatures
whose reaching is less an apparent manifestation,
and upon whom the shadows of impression are cast,
There,
There is luxury.

And when spectrum,
array,
and infinite variety
blend amongst turbulent vapor
and chemical luminescence,
while only eyes reach toward them
these are yet

gnarled, naked, and frozen
and this simply the interaction betwixt the classes
between whom the shadows of impression are unidirectional.
There,
There is superiority of luxury.

Haiku
Mary Galligan

(5-7-5 syllable Haiku)
(Created while viewing from the train the olive trees
with silver colored bark in groves at Le Oce, Italy.)

Silver sentinels,
Dark trunks woven by ancient
Fingers of hot wind.

Undertaking
Kaye Yadusky

Haiku
6 lines

Laboring, salmon
Contest the river rapids,
Irresistibly drawn

Toward a sinking sun
Dyeing the water, crimson
Is the child's first cry.

The Ash Tree
Kaye Yadusky

(Written in Free Verse)
29 lines
(Elaeagnus = silverberry = oleaster = Russian olive =
wild olive is a genus of 50 to 70 flowering plants
native to Asia, but mostly cultivated in China.)

She waits,
while the orchestra warms up; fragments of yellow greening
themes
pitch and catch, here then there, across the amphitheater,
pauses, then swells into a symphony of summer foliage,
spring onion, babies breath, Elaeagnus, white barked birch.

She is quiet,
while the orchestra climaxes in a showy Offenbach of blue, bottle-
bottom green,
then everywhere a prolonged-beyond-patience, stifling, languid,
when can we leave, 17th century proper parlor piece dénouement.
Long lanky weeds flourish; drying grass begs for rain.

She listens,
when comes the suggestion of approaching parade, a singular
brown note crows red;
a small brass band starts up a march and ushers in a Mardi Gras,
singing, shouting, chanting, laughing, intoxicating, flaming,
yellows, reds, oranges, closing windows, smoking chimneys.

She dims,
when a cold, rain-driven, grey wind assaults and strips the
amphitheater bare,
revealing its shadowy scaffolding, stretching, aspiring,
heavenward,
abandoned, echoing...

But she clings

tenaciously to her paper-bag brown leaves even as the elements
bleach and beat
her adornment thinner and lighter, and press her limbs to precious
metal,

Until she becomes
insect wings of golden gossamer suspended from wisps of
titanium,

Laughing with the winter wind,
Chatting gaily
Singing in the silence,
A solo artist,
The Ash Tree.

Interview
Aleksandra Yadusky

(Written in Free Verse)
6 lines

Nice pants
Cold sweats
I think about all the pressure
Coal must feel
Just knowing
It could be a diamond.

Untitled-1

Alexandra Yadusky

(Written in Free Verse)
25 lines

Sometimes,
Your heart will be heavy, and lonely;
The weight of the world on your shoulders.
And you won't believe me, but
I was just like you.
I felt those things too.

There were other times, too,
When I was having a blast
Spending time with friends, just being me.
I gave up running the show, and amazing things happened.
People loved me, all of me, and I remembered how to love back.
It felt so good, even knowing it wasn't forever.
I was finally real,
And I got to see you feel real too.

I went sailing, and I remembered so much about myself.
The wind in my hair, the sun's white light on the water,
and a sense of weightlessness.
I felt it, all the way through me,
It was so Zen.
And then, again, I felt it,
when the wind changed, and it grew dark so quickly
I couldn't tell the sun from the sky.
But I let go of my fear.
And it was as if something spoke to me, on the inside,
Saying, "Peace, be still."

Untitled-2
Aleksandra Yadusky

(Written in Free Verse)
6 lines

Tiny life,
Little god
Just coming to
In the world again,
Does something deep in you remember colors
Or the sense of touch?

Sweet Dreams

Megan Yadusky   age 11

Sleep my child.
Do not wake up.
Morning is mild,
Before your day is up.

Dream sweet one
From lands near and far,
Like frosting on a cinnamon bun.
Yes, you are dreaming, and that's who you are.

One day in a land far away
On a beautiful day of May
There is a castle that lay
Where a prince and princess are married to this very day

Where swords are fought with kings and knights
In the glorious stars of the beautiful night
With shields, plates, and horses galore
I can see the child's love forever more

Sleep my child
Morning is near
Sleep my child
And now you are here

Baby Birds

Megan Yadusky   age 13

(Written in a meter of ..-.-)
A trimeter of one anapest and two iambic feet
20 rhyming lines

I awakened to the nest,
After a long winter's rest,
For the tweets of all the birds
By my ear they could be heard.
    And I took a peak inside
    At what mother made with pride.
    There were many furry friends,
    And their tweets did never end.
I looked down into the nest
Where the little birds did rest.
When they're fed their cries let out,
And it made them scream and shout.
    She did her daily routine,
    Feeding at seven-fifteen.
    And the nest is much cluttered,
    Where the birds are all mothered.
They will soon be on their way
To a great bird air display
In the heavens up above,
Flying peacefully like doves.

Moon Tales
Scott Yadusky

(Written in Free Verse)
15 lines

When our fiery sun quiets,
the cool moon speaks.

Then, minds open with
night's mysterious tale.

A tale of earth bursting
porous fruits.

Celestial spice flavoring
deep roots,

then, ink up paper
with Western King bird's decree
pinned to every tree.

Nature's blueprint hallmarks
our fiery sunrise gratis.

Daylight discovers
night's "mysterious tale!"

Recipe for a Peaceful Moment
Ann Barta

(Written in Free Verse)
41 lines

(Ann says this moment happened while she and her brother John attended NCSU as undergraduates. He was the RA or the resident assistant, and he roomed with Bobby Pham on the first floor in a room with stereo sound. And Ann was living right upstairs on the "girls-only" third floor, at Alexander International dormitory, with many other wonderful friends like Beth Yow, Evelyn Moreno, Lai Lei Ng, Anna Suarez, Jaime Widener, and others. One time, John told Ann about his being up so late studying and being so tired that he fell asleep in (calculus?) class, and he started snoring and drooling on the desk. He couldn't believe it, but not even one student woke him up! (Don't you think, maybe, no one from Alexander was in that class?) Too late, the professor noticed and got John wide awake!! It was the first and last time that John let that happen.)

Once my big brother took my arm and said,
"Come.
Come listen to something.
Come with me into this darkened room with the stereo,
sit down
and let's watch the music flicker together
like a campfire,
the treble,
the bass,
tiny yellow-orange lights
dancing up and down,
dancing to this mellow peaceful
Christian song."
It was like Jesus' whisper to us,
"You are loved.
I've got your back.
I've got a room for you in your real home,
your heavenly home,
so do not be afraid;

do not be anxious.
Close your eyes for awhile,
or just watch the lights
in their synchrony with the melody
and let yourself rest awhile."
You know, sometimes I just
lie here
in the dark,
and watch the lights
or close my eyes,
as I listen and soak in the music,
as I rest and quiet my soul,
and open to the presence of God.
Wow.
Thanks John.

Psalm 139
Where can I go from your Spirit?
Where can I flee from your presence?
...If I rise on the wings of the dawn,
if I settle on the far side of the sea,
even there your hand will guide me,
your right hand will hold me fast.

For My Teachers Who Are So Amazing!
Stephanie Cessna

(Written in a meter of ..-..-..-)
Anapest Trimeter
9 syllables in 12 rhyming lines

(Stephanie says that she wrote this poem at the end of
elementary school to be put into a card for the special
education teachers of her autistic son, Hunter.)

If I could talk, I would surely say,
"Thanks for helping me in every way."
Also thanks for teaching me to see
That there's many things that I can be.
No matter how big or small my task,
Even if I cannot seem to ask,
You push and guide and keep me in line.
Teachers are absolutely divine!
And thanks for helping me understand
That the world around me is quite grand.
When I'm grown, I will always think too
That "Excellent Teachers" do mean: You!

Baseball
Jacob Yadusky   age 8

4 rhyming lines

When you play baseball
You can trip and fall
You can throw a ball into the hall
With the ball which is small